Balance sheet structures

ACT

THE ASSOCIATION OF CORPORATE TREASURERS

The Association is a professional body, formed to encourage and promote the study and practice of finance and treasury management, and to educate those involved in this field. It is the only UK professional body which concentrates and sets professional examinations exclusively on this subject. It is an independent body, governed by a Council of Members whose work is supported by a number of active voluntary committees.

The Association has approximately 3000 members and more than 1300 professionals enrolled on examination courses.

Since its formation in 1979, the influence of and contribution made by the Association has grown steadily. High educational standards have fed through into high technical standards. This has meant that, as an organization, the Association focuses not only on serving its members directly, but also representing them on relevant issues in the public domain. It has influenced proposals for regulatory change and promoted voluntary codes for wholesale market participants. It has also influenced changes in accounting and tax legislation. The Association has contributed to the corporate governance debate and aspects of competition policy, and has been consulted on and successfully contributed to many practical aspects of European Monetary Union. These messages are reinforced at conferences and in the publications it produces.

Balance sheet structures

Edited by Anthony Birts

WOODHEAD PUBLISHING LIMITED

and

THE ASSOCIATION OF CORPORATE TREASURERS

Published by Woodhead Publishing Limited and The Association of Corporate Treasurers
Woodhead Publishing Limited, Abington Hall, Abington
Cambridge CB1 6AH, England
www.woodhead-publishing.com

First published 2001, Woodhead Publishing Ltd and The Association of Corporate Treasurers

British Library Cataloguing in Publication Data
A catalogue record for this book is available from the British Library.

ISBN 1 85573 247 5

Cover design by The ColourStudio
Typeset by Best-set Typesetter Ltd., Hong Kong
Printed by TJ International Ltd, Cornwall, England

To Libby

Contents

List of contributors

Chapters 1, 2, 4 and 6 Anthony Birts
Anthony N Birts BSc, MBA, Cert CM is currently Teaching Fellow in Finance at the School of Management, University of Bath and is also Director of the MBA Programmes. Having started out in a manufacturing company, in various roles ranging from shop floor supervisor to assistant to the Marketing Director, after three years he left to do an MBA at the Manchester Business School. He then joined Bank of America NT & SA, initially in the Energy Section as an Account Officer, ending up as a Vice President in the Global Payments section based in London. He left the Bank in 1989 to join Bath University.

Chapter 3 Stephen J East
Stephen J East, having trained as a Chartered Accountant, joined Redland PLC's treasury department in 1983 becoming group treasurer in 1987. Having established a corporate finance consultancy business he joined MEPC plc as Director of Corporate Finance in 1997 and was appointed Finance Director in 1999. Stephen is currently a Vice President of The Association of Corporate Treasurers having previously chaired its publications, programme and education committees.

Chapter 3 case study Michael MacCallan
Michael MacCallan BA, FCA, FCT, is Vice President and Treasurer, Esselte AB, the Swedish global office supplies company. During his career he has had extensive senior international management experience gained in the treasury, controller and credit functions of major corporations including Del Monte Foods International, Cookson Group plc, Engelhard Corporation and Gulf Oil Corporation. He is a Chartered Accountant, having qualified with Price Waterhouse. Michael is author of *Re-engineering corporate treasury* (ACT Business of Finance series) and is a contributor to *Managing banking relationships* (Woodhead Publishing Limited). He is a regular contributor to

a wide range of specialist financial publications and also lectures on treasury issues at international conferences and seminars.

Chapter 4 case study Gary Couch

Gary Couch is Finance Director of the Avebury Group, a group which owns and operates approximately 700 tenanted pubs throughout England and Wales. Together with three others, he founded Avebury in 1997, since which time the company has grown to become one of the country's largest independent pub operators. He qualified as a chartered accountant with Arthur Andersen in London and subsequently worked for Chemical Bank prior to joining Household Mortgage Corporation.

Chapter 5 and case study Anthony Stern

Anthony Stern is Director of Treasury at Bass PLC, which he joined in 1988. His responsibilities cover treasury and banking matters over the ninety countries in which the group deals through its Inter-Continental and Holiday Inn hotels. He was educated at Oxford University and the Manchester Business School (MBS) and it was at MBS that he met Anthony Birts.

Chapter 5 case study Tim Owen

Tim Owen is Director of Treasury at Cadbury Schweppes plc, a UK company with a turnover of £4bn and a market capitalisation of over £8bn. He has spent his entire career with Cadbury Schweppes, initially in various management accounting roles, moving into treasury in 1989. He was appointed to his current position in 1995.

Chapter 7 Alan Clements and Moody's New Instruments Standing Committee

After a spell in the Inland Revenue as a Tax Inspector, Alan Clements joined ICI in 1956, becoming Treasurer in 1976. He joined the Main Board in 1979 and was responsible for Finance and other areas until 1990. He has also served on several other boards – David S Smith (Holdings) (Chairman); MGN plc (Deputy Chairman); Cable & Wireless; Granada; Trafalgar House (Chairman); Brent Walker; Cementone plc (Chairman); and Guinness Mahon Holdings plc. He was the Founder President of The Association of Corporate Treasurers.

Moody's New Instruments Standing Committee: (New York) Brian Clarkson, Kent Becker, Tim Blake, Rosemarie Conforte, Patrick Finnegan, Barbara Havlicek, Tom Marshella, Ryan O'Connell, Farisa Zarin; (London) Nicholas Holmes.

Preface

This book has been written with a number of objectives in mind. First and foremost, it aims to provide a practical guide to balance sheet issues for a wide group of potentially interested parties – treasurers, bankers, directors and students of business and economics. To this end, the book covers a modicum of financial theory relating to the debt versus equity issue. The purpose of this is threefold: firstly, for completeness; secondly, because financial theory does help to focus attention upon the important factors that need to be taken into account, even if answers cannot be provided with quite the precision suggested by the theories, and even if some of the basic assumptions appear unrealistic; thirdly, to provide a sounding-board against which the actions of the financial decision makers can be tested and understood.

The main body of the book is given over to the practical, and tries to answer the questions:

- Why do companies have balance sheets structured as they are?
- Do industry differences rule the structure?
- Does a multinational differ greatly from a domestic company?
- Does management's attitude to risk have any effect?

These questions are looked at through a series of case studies, in the most part written by those who are responsible for the balance sheet structures they are living with. The second aim is to help the reader understand the interrelationship between debt and equity in terms of the overall value of the company and the impact on the company's cost of capital. Thirdly, the aim is to describe the various elements that go to make up the balance sheet, and the costs and benefits that attach to each. Fourthly, the aim is to describe the interrelationship between the business that the company is in, the maximisation of cash flows and the balance sheet that matches the business reality. Where relevant, further reading will be referenced for those interested in pursuing some issues in more depth.

A number of decisions need to be made by the financial manager with respect to the objective of maximising shareholders' wealth. In no particular order of importance, these include:

- capital budgeting and the decision as to which competing projects the company should undertake;
- calculating the company's correct cost of capital, in particular that of equity;
- the dividend decision;
- working capital management;
- cash and liquidity management;
- financing the company and the split between debt and equity, and within these two broad areas, the types of instrument available.

It is the latter issue that this book seeks to address, although, as all the decisions are interrelated, they will be touched on wherever appropriate. Before starting, it is worth stating that in this book the two terms 'gearing' and 'leverage' will be used interchangeably to describe the process when a company takes debt into its balance sheet, i.e. a company that is solely equity financed could be referred to as unleveraged or ungeared. The capital of a company usually refers to the long-term funds invested in a company, i.e. debt with a maturity over a year, and equity.

The structure of the book follows this intermixing of theory and practice. This is designed so that, as the reader progresses, he/she can pick up the themes that are common in both theory and practice and be able to see the different slant that is put on common issues, depending on the writer's perspective and background.

Chapters 1 and 2 form a theoretical base and look at the academic interpretation of the empirical evidence on how companies structure their balance sheets. Chapters 3, 4 and 5 are all written by practitioners. Chapter 3 takes a broad look at the issue of the types of instruments available and how they might fit together. Chapter 4 develops on Chapter 3 with a practical approach to structuring a balance sheet. Chapter 5 then adds the international dimension to the domestic considerations that have been the main focus until now. Chapter 6 looks at the theory behind the dividend decision, while Chapter 7 considers the external issues of the company managing the communication of its rationale for the financing structure it has chosen to the outside world.

The case studies are intended to illustrate the kind of decision processes that companies go through in reality. To this end, what they say was important to them, whether or not it maps neatly onto the theory or others' view of what is important. The book carries the usual caveat that tax rates and other market information should be viewed as illustrative only and should not be relied upon to determine actions in today's markets, even though every effort has been made to ensure that they were accurate at the time of writing.

Thanks are due to Andrew McMillan, Head of Insurance at The Royal Bank of Scotland plc and Arun Shankardass, Group Treasury Manager at CGNU plc, for their valuable input at various stages.

It is hoped that the book will help in aiding financial managers' thought processes and in deciding which factors are important at any one time, rather than pretending that there are any universally correct answers.

Chapter

1 Debt versus equity

Introduction

There are a number of important financial decisions to be made in trying to attain a company's objective of maximising shareholders' wealth or, where this is not the main objective, of maximising the utilisation of resources. How to finance the company is just one of these, but nonetheless an important one. While we must recognise that it is not a decision that sits on its own, unrelated to what is going on elsewhere, it is still worthwhile giving it consideration in some depth and then bringing in the other factors. The first thing we need to consider is whether it is in fact an important decision, because, if mixing debt and equity in different proportions does not affect share value, managers should not spend any further time on that decision and should rather concentrate on more important issues. If, on the other hand, it is seen to be important, managers will wish to know what factors they should be taking into account. There is no need to reinvent the wheel here, as there are plenty of existing companies whose example can be followed if it makes sense and if the factors that drove those companies decisions are similar to the ones important in the current situation. First, however, we need to consider just what the company wishes to do.

Purpose of the firm

In traditional financial theory, the overall objective of the firm and, hence, all those employed by the firm is a simple one, namely to maximise shareholders' wealth. Another way of putting this is that management's aim is to maximise share value, since the value of a share at any one time should represent the present value of all future cash flows flowing to the investor from their investment. That is, the flow of dividends plus any terminal value, discounted at the correct risk-adjusted discount rate.

Most textbooks sensibly include other objectives as well. For example, from a shareholder's point of view, issues such as the environment and ethics can be so important that a more environmentally friendly, but more expensive, production process may be preferred even though it shows a lower rate of return compared with a less environmentally friendly process. (Sophisticated cost benefit/utility analysis may be able to quantify these benefits and thus enable such issues to be brought into the wealth-maximisation equation.)

Other interests are also recognised, such as the objectives of managers and other employees. These are not always in line with those of the shareholders. For example, management may see a strong correlation between size of company and size of salary. In consequence, the management may go all out for growth, perhaps via an expensive marketing drive and advertising campaign. In this instance, growth may be obtained at the expense of profit. Another route may be the acquisition trail, and again this can result in reduced earnings per share or slower growth. Subjective issues, such as size of office, may also be important. Is it large enough to have the desk in a diagonal position for instance! These sorts of issues, which may not be minor in human terms, can add to overheads.

From the perspective of the employees, continued employment at maximum wages may be their hearts' desire, in which case they may prefer to see older, less efficient, manufacturing processes remain in place rather than see newer, more sophisticated, more efficient processes introduced, which boost productivity but which need less labour.

There are many more examples where the objectives of the players involved are contradictory. This dilemma, the separation of management and ownership, has given rise to a number of theories as to how the shareholders can ensure that their interests are kept to the fore. These range from agency theory (see also Chapter 7) to theories that apply the power and discipline of the market place.

Agency theory looks at the ways in which the shareholders are able to 'police' their managers' actions through the use of auditors and other methods, such as the Annual General Meeting. There is obviously a cost to the shareholders involved in doing this, so that the extreme of monitoring every action of the management is not feasible, since the cost of doing so would reduce overall wealth. Similarly, the other extreme of doing nothing is also seen as too costly. The compromise is the annual audit of varying degrees of thoroughness, professionalism and cost.

The market-place approach assumes that the market will be monitoring the performance of the management. If they are not seen to be performing adequately and making good use of the assets in their charge, then the price of the shares will fall, predators will move in, the firm will be acquired and the management removed. How efficiently either of these methods works is open to debate, but what can probably be agreed is that no one, be they shareholders, managers or employees, wishes to see the firm cease to trade. Because of this, their actions will be to a greater or lesser extent aimed at creating wealth, even if they do not aim to maximise it. From a financial management standpoint, while recognising the push and pull of these issues, it is nonetheless simplest to hold on to the basic aim of the firm, and hence financial management, as being to maximise shareholders' wealth. It is within this framework that the debt/equity decision is examined.

The theory

The debate simply put is as follows: can the management of a company affect its overall value, by varying the proportions of debt and equity in its total capital? By overall value, we mean the total value to both debt holders and equity holders. For those who like a simple equation, the question can be posed as follows: what happens to K_0 (the weighted average cost of capital) as the proportions of equity and debt are changed?

$$K_0 = K_e\left(\frac{E}{E+D}\right) + K_d\left(\frac{D}{E+D}\right)$$

where K_0 is the weighted average cost of capital, K_e is the cost of equity, K_d is the cost of debt, E is the amount of equity finance, and D is the amount of debt finance.

Broadly there were two lines of argument. On the one hand there were those who said that whatever the proportion of E and D, K_0 stayed the same. In other words, the company produced an economic return, or cake, and no matter how you sliced the cake between debt and equity holders, the total cake stayed the same. This is referred to as the net operating approach and can be illustrated as in Table 1.1.

Of course, there is always room for an opposing view and this was supplied by another group referred to as the Modern Traditionalists. The Modern Traditionalists said the opposite, namely that, yes, the total value of the company could be altered by varying the proportions of debt and equity, as illustrated in Fig. 1.1. As the proportion of debt to equity is altered, this will result in a lower overall average cost of capital. This in turn will result in a higher value of the company for any given level of net operating income (NOI). At point A in Fig. 1.1, the weighted cost of capital equals 15%, for an NOI of £1 000 000. This gives the value of £6 666 666. (£1 000 000/0.15 = £6 666 666, or to put it another way, at an interest rate

Table 1.1 The net operating approach

	Structure 1	**Structure 2**
Net operating income	1000	1000
Overall capitalisation rate (K_0)	0.16	0.16
Total value of the firm*	6250	6250
Market value of debt (Interest rate 100/0)	1000	4000
Market value of equity (total value less debt)	5250	2250
Earnings to shareholders	900	600
Rate of return to shareholders (Earnings to shareholders) (Value of equity)	17.14	26.67

Note: Although the return to shareholders increases, the total value of the company remains at 6250.

* Total value $= \frac{1000}{0.16}$ or at a rate of interest of 16%, £6250 invested now will give £1000 per annum to perpetuity.

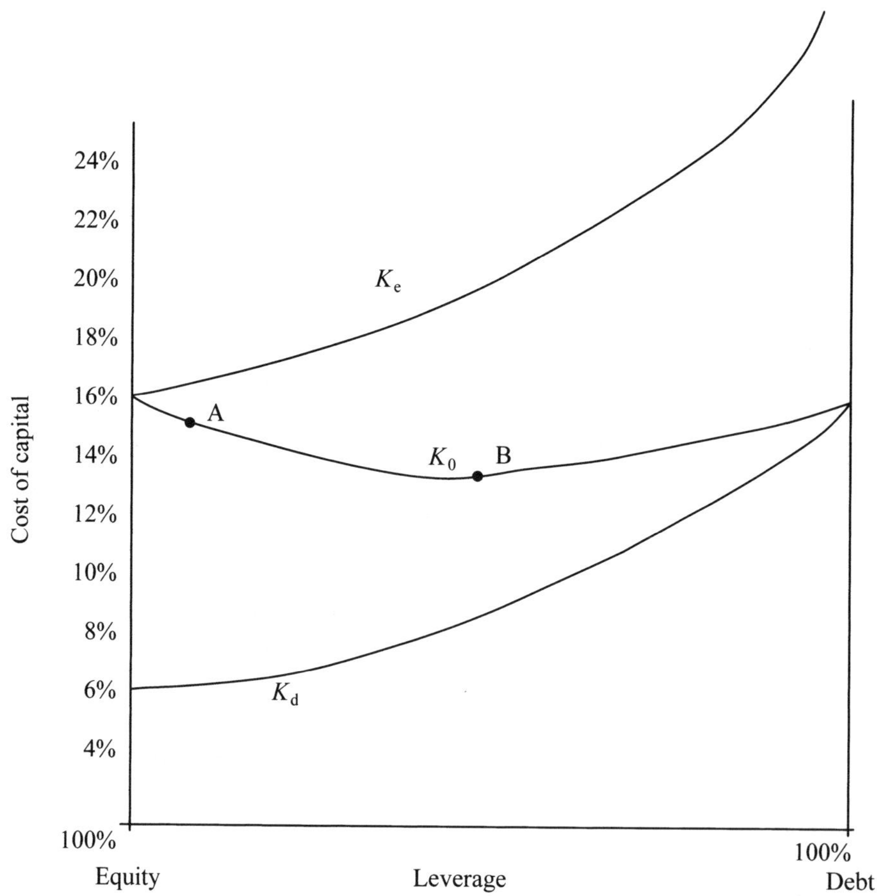

1.1 Traditional approach: judicious use of leverage will increase the value of the firm.

Table 1.2 Deriving the average cost of capital curve, an illustration

Percentage of debt and equity in total capital	Cost of debt and equity, %	Weighted average cost of capital, %
All equity	16	16
90 Equity	16.1	14.5
10 Debt	6.0	0.6
		15.1
75 Equity	17.0	12.75
25 Debt	6.0	1.50
		14.25
50 Equity	21	10.50
50 Debt	7	3.50
		14.00*
40 Equity	23	9.2
60 Debt	9	5.4
		14.2
30 Equity	26	7.8
70 Debt	11	7.7
		15.5

* Minimum cost of capital.

level of 15% an investor would be willing to invest £6 666 666 to give an annual income of £1 000 000.) At point B, the K_0 is roughly 13%, which gives a value of £7 692 308. Table 1.2 illustrates the sort of numbers that will give rise to the total average cost curve as illustrated in Fig. 1.1.

The thinking behind Table 1.2 is that, as debt is introduced, the cost of equity immediately begins to rise as the risk increases, but that initially the cost of debt does not. As the proportion of debt increases, the debt holders start to recognise that they are taking on too much of the total risk of the company and therefore start to demand a higher rate of return commensurate with the risk that they have taken on. This results in an optimal debt equity mix of around 50/50 in this example.

The discussion continued until Modigliani and Miller (1969) produced their arbitrage proof of the net operating approach. This proof was based on the thought that, in a perfect market, two companies producing the same economic benefit should be valued the same. If they are not, then investors will be able to make risk-free gains by switching from one company to the other. Neither would a company be able to do anything that a shareholder could not do for himself, so no value should be given to the company for doing something that the shareholders could do themselves, for example, borrowing money when a shareholder is able to borrow for himself. Shareholders will switch from one company to the other if companies are valued

Table 1.3 Arbitrage support proof for the NOI approach

	Company A	Company B
NOI	1 000 000	1 000 000
Interest on debt	–	330 000
Earnings to shareholders	1 000 000	670 000
Cost of equity	0.13	0.134
Market value of equity	7 692 308	5 000 000
Market value of debt	–	3 000 000
Total value of the company	7 692.308	8 000 000
K_0	13%	12.5%
An investor in company B with 2% of the shares has:		
a share value of	100 000	
and earnings of	13 400	
Investor in company B could		
(1) Sell shares in B for	100 000	
(2) Borrow 2% of B's debt	60 000	
to give total funds of	160 000	
(3) Invest in 2% of company A	153 846	
Funds left over	6 154	
(4) Earnings from company A	20 000 (2% of 1 000 000)	
(5) Interest cost	6 600	
(6) Net earnings	13 400	

The shareholder is able to duplicate the actions of company B and make the same return, as if he had remained in company B, of 13 400 but still have funds left over of 6154.

differently, until their values are equal. Table 1.3 illustrates this process where company A has no debt and company B has debt of 3 000 000.

The end result of all the actions undertaken by a shareholder moving from company B to company A is to have the same net earnings as a shareholder in company B but for an outlay of £6154 less. This could be invested in further shares of company A, showing an additional return of £800. If one shareholder can do this, so might all shareholders. This activity will continue until the values of the companies equalise as the price of B is pushed down and the price of A is pushed up. Appendix 1.1 shows the effect when there is the same amount and cost of debt for B, but cost of equity is 13.834 for B and 12.75 for A.

While the proof is very neat, the reader will have noticed that it is based on the assumption of a perfect capital market. The major assumptions within this are:

- Information is costless and freely available.
- Investors are rational.

- Securities are divisible.
- No transaction costs.
- No corporate taxes.
- No costs of bankruptcy.

But the world is not a perfect place, and all the assumptions can be criticised to a greater or lesser extent. We now need to look at them and see what effect changing those assumptions may have on the theory.

The effect of imperfections

We need not spend too much time on many of these assumptions. Information, for instance, is not costless and different levels of information are more, or less, available to different classes of investor. However, it is surprising just how much information is available these days, seemingly free, even to the private investor via the Internet. As for the professional institutional investors, they should have access to as much information as any other institution in the same business, although the quality of their analysis and the accuracy of their predictions will no doubt still depend on the skill of the individual involved. The problem of asymmetry of information between those inside the company and those outside will still remain, but at least one could argue that, for the investors, it is more or less a level playing field.

This leads into the issue of the rationality of investors. The term 'rational' here really means that most investors are risk averse. This in turn does not mean that investors will not take on risk, but that for any increase in the perceived risk of one investment over another, they will expect a higher rate of return. It does not necessarily mean that investors will take a decision that appears rational to everyone else. Tobacco companies may show a good rate of return for the risk involved, but there are plenty of investors who will not invest in them on ethical grounds.

The divisibility of securities would be important if the value of a share was very large and an exact replication was necessary to achieve a perfect arbitrage. In a market with relatively low share prices, such as the UK, this would not cause a problem. Perhaps if you are the proud owner of a Berkshire Hathaway share, with a high in 1999 of $81 100, then divisibility might become an issue.

As far as transaction costs are concerned, we know that there is a cost involved in buying and selling shares. These costs are relatively low these days even for the small investor (£2.50 to buy as a minimum commission via one Internet company) and, while they would cause a barrier to perfect arbitrage, are not a major issue.

The really serious imperfections relate to the last two items: tax and bankruptcy.

In a perfect, tax-free world, as shown above, there is no advantage in terms of the total value of the company in worrying about debt to equity proportions. However, since tax most certainly does exist for most companies to a greater or lesser degree, we need to focus on the effect that this has on the debt/equity decision. The basic argument adopted by the NOI proponents is that the company is a cake, and no matter how the cake is sliced between debt and equity, the size of the cake is still the same. While this is true, we now have to invite a third (unwelcome) guest to the party, namely the Government. Now the party game can become one of making the slices for the equity and debt holders as large as possible, while leaving the Government as small a slice as possible.

We can look at this problem and its effects on rates of return on two levels. The first level looks at the effects of tax and debt at what could be termed the absolute figure level. The second level introduces the idea of the varying levels of risk that are introduced, by varying debt-to-equity levels, to the parties involved and seeing whether this affects the rate of return required by each party and, hence, the ultimate valuation of their holdings. The costs of bankruptcy will be dealt with at that time.

Effects at the absolute figure level

The net effect of tax will depend on the way tax is applied. Implicit in the following analysis is the convention that interest on debt is deducted from earnings before tax and that dividends are paid out of net after-tax income.

It can be seen from Table 1.4 that by introducing debt into the company the total income has increased from £600 000 to £720 000, while the rate of return on equity (RoE) has risen from 12% to 16.8%. Suppose that in the all-equity example, 5 000 000 shares with a nominal value of £1.00 each represent the £5 000 000 of capital. The net present value (NPV) of the current net income flows (assuming no growth) is £5 000 000. The NPV represents the amount an investor would be willing to pay today to secure an income of £600 000 per year in perpetuity at a rate of return of 12%. This would give a current market value to the shares of £5 000 000/5 000 000 or £1. If we pursue the same analysis for the debt equity example, the share price increases. The NPV to equity is £3 500 000 represented by 2 500 000 shares or a value of £1.40 per share.

At this stage then, we can say that using debt, where interest is deductible from income before tax, has increased the value of the firm. The extra value is derived from the Government's subsidising the company's interest bill by an amount equal to the corporate tax rate. This 'subsidy' is referred to as the tax shield. The annual value of the tax shield is equal to the amount of debt interest times the effective corporate tax rate (debt interest × corporate tax

Table 1.4 Rate of return increases with leverage

ABC Company		
Total capital	£5 000 000	
Operating income	£1 000 000	
Corporate tax rate	40%	
Cost of debt	12%	
	All equity financed	50% debt financed
Operating income	£1 000 000	£1 000 000
Debt interest	–	£300 000*
NOI	£1 000 000	£700 000
Tax at 40%	£400 000	£280 000
Net income	£600 000	£420 000
RoE	12%	16.8%
EPS†	12p	16.8p
Total income to:		
equity	£600 000	£420 000
debt	–	£300 000
Total income	£600 000	£720 000
Difference	£120 000	
which equals debt interest	× tax rate	
300 000	× 0.40	= £120 000

* £2 500 000 × 0.12 = £300 000.
† EPS stands for earnings per share.

Table 1.5 Present value of tax shield

	All equity financed	**50% debt financed**
Net present value to equity holders (Assuming no change in required rate of return)	$\frac{600\,000}{0.12} = 5\,000\,000$	$\frac{420\,000}{0.12} = 3\,500\,000$
Net present value to debt holders	–	$\frac{300\,000}{0.12} = 2\,500\,000$
Total value of the company	5 000 000	6 000 000
Difference	1 000 000	
which equals present value of tax benefit	$\frac{120\,000}{0.12} = 1\,000\,000$	
	or 2 500 000 × 0.4 = 1 000 000	

rate). The net present value of this is normally derived by dividing this amount by the debt interest rate. Another way of deriving the NPV of the tax shield is simply to multiply the total amount of debt by the corporate tax rate. (Annual tax shield value = $D \times r_d \times t_c$ where D is the amount of debt, r_d is the interest rate of debt, and t_c is the corporate tax rate. The NPV of annual tax shield = $D \times r_d \times t_c / r_d$, or $D \times t_c$, assuming debt is used in perpetuity.) The calculations for ABC Co are given in Table 1.5.

Given the benefit of debt, the obvious solution is to borrow as much as possible until all the tax benefit is used up; in this case, borrow £8 333 333, or rather more than the company needs. This would produce an interest cost of £1 000 000 (assuming that the rate does not increase over 12%), which uses up all the taxable income. The last shareholder to leave the building can afford to leave the light on.

Since this 'logical' solution is obviously ridiculous (even if appealing), there must be some problem with it. The first problem relates to what the shareholders and debt holders are ultimately interested in, i.e. a 'net after all taxes' return to them. In other words, the analysis so far has looked only at the effect of taxes at the corporate level; we need to include taxes at the personal level as well.

The net income received by the debt holder will have only personal taxes deducted; in other words the original one pound of operating income paid to them without corporate tax deducted, only tax on debt income (t_d) deducted, i.e. $I - t_d$. The receiver of equity income who is a tax payer, however, will receive a net dividend from the net income that is left after corporate taxes (t_c) have been deducted. He will therefore pay personal taxes on equity income (t_e) on the net after corporate tax income, i.e. $(I - t_c)t_e$, so that the total tax paid on equity income is $I - t_c - t_e(I - t_c)$ or $(I - t_e)(I - t_c)$. The decision as to which route, debt or equity, will give the greatest overall after-tax return will be driven by the relationship between the respective tax rates. From a total value point of view, where $I - t_d = (I - t_e)(I - t_c)$, the company becomes indifferent as to how much debt or how much equity it should use. This is illustrated in Table 1.6 using the same company parameters as in Table 1.4, but adding debt and equity taxes.

It can be seen that, within a wide range of debt/equity ratios, the total value of flows to debt and equity holders does not vary. Where $I - t_d$ is less than $(I - t_e)(I - t_c)$, however, it is advantageous to increase equity. Where $I - t_d$ is greater than $(I - t_e)(I - t_c)$, there is an advantage in having more debt. This is illustrated in Table 1.7.

This analysis leaves us open to debate, since the decision as to where a company lies depends on (i) its own effective corporate tax rate, (ii) the tax rate on receivers of debt interest, and (iii) the tax rate on receivers of equity income. As the marginal rates of tax of all a company's shareholders and debt holders probably vary, deciding on what 'the rate' is will be problematic. A question therefore posed at this point is whether or not financial managers consider the individual tax positions of the various stakeholders in making their leverage decisions. We shall see what they say later. A worse problem, however, is the one that we have already encountered, which is that, where it is advantageous to leverage the company, then the implication is that maximum value will be derived where the company is leveraged to the hilt. Patently, we do not see companies in general behaving like this and so we must look further for reasons why not.

Table 1.6 Effect of tax levels on net return in equilibrium

Corporate tax rate (t_c)	= 40%			
Tax on debt income (t_d)	= 50%			
Tax on equity income (t_e)	= 16.6666 (taken to 16.66)			
note ($l - t_d$)	= ($l - t_e$)($l - t_c$)			
0.5	= 0.833334 × 0.6			
1 50% debt 50% equity				
	'£'			
Operating income	1 000 000			
Debt interest (12%)	300 000			
Pre-tax income	700 000			
Corporate tax (t_c) 40%	280 000			'£'
Net corporate earnings (NCE)	420 000			300 000
t_e @ 16.66	69 972		t_d @ 50%	150 000
Net to shareholder/debtholder	350 028		+	150 000
			=	500 028
2 30% debt 70% equity				
	'£'			
Operating income	1 000 000			
Debt interest (12%)	180 000			
Pre-tax income	820 000			
t_c	328 000			
NCE	492 000			180 000
t_e	81 967		t_d	90 000
Net to shareholder/debtholder	410 033		+	90 000
			=	500 033
3 70% debt 30% equity				
	'£'			
Operating income	1 000 000			
Debt interest (12%)	420 000			
Pre-tax income	580 000			
t_c	232 000			
NCE	348 000			420 000
t_e	57 977		t_d	210 000
Net to shareholder/debtholder	290 023		+	210 000
			=	500 023

Table 1.7 Effect of tax levels/disequilibrium

Tax	Rate	l – tax rate	($l - t_e$)($l - t_c$)	Values of combined flows at D/E of 50/50	40/60
t_c	25%	0.75 }	0.62505	587 535	595 038
t_e	16.66%	0.8334 }			
t_d	50%	0.5		$l - t_d < (l - t_e)(l - t_c)$ (0.5) < (0.63505)	More debt lower total
t_c	40%	0.6 }	0.50004	530 003	524 003
t_e	16.66%	0.8334 }			
t_d	40%	0.6		$l - t_d > (l - t_e)(l - t_c)$ (0.6) > (0.5004)	More debt higher total

To summarise so far, though, before we continue:

- In a perfect world the debt/equity decision is of no importance.
- But the world is not perfect, and a major imperfection is tax.
- Where a company is paying tax, there is an advantage in leveraging up the company to increase total flows from the company.
- Personal taxes may be important as it is the total net of tax flows that debt and equity holders are interested in.
- Therefore, where debt is favoured by the tax regime, the company should borrow the maximum amount possible.

Effect on risk and required rates of return

It is now time to consider the second level mentioned earlier, that is the question of increasing risk and its effect on required rates of return.

In financial terms, risk is the chance that the outcome will not be as expected. We may expect a return of 15% from an equity investment, but it could be 10% or 20%, depending on a number of issues. The greater the potential variability, the greater the risk. The total risk of a company can be divided into business risk and financial risk. (The distinction between diversifiable and undiversifiable risk is made later.) Business risk derives from the nature of the business itself, e.g. bioengineering is less predictable than producing basic foodstuffs. Financial risk, on the other hand, is a result of the way in which a company chooses to finance itself.

Increasing levels of debt are usually seen as increasing the risk to equity holders. This is due to the fact that, while dividend payments do not have to be made in a year in which there is a shortfall of cash, interest payments on debt do have to be paid. Failure to pay interest when due may lead to breaches of covenant and bankruptcy. In a bankruptcy, equity holders are unlikely to receive all of their capital, since a very different valuation is put on assets in a forced sale from that in a going concern. There are also costs involved in the process of bankruptcy, both directly and indirectly. Direct costs would be solicitors' and accountants' fees. An example of an indirect cost could be the distraction of management attention from running the business while fire-fighting. In addition, in the run up to a bankruptcy, it is likely that the market will be reading the signals and reacting to them. Suppliers will reduce their credit terms, perhaps demanding payment against delivery rather than extending credit for 60 days (or cease to supply at all), and customers worried about service will take flight. At the same time, the suppliers of debt will be raising the cost of debt. All this means that there is a definite cost in financial distress involved as well as bankruptcy (or fighting it off). This will reduce the net amount available for distribution to shareholders.

The increased chance of bankruptcy lowers the NPV of the value of the company. Suppose that the NPV of bankruptcy costs is £1 000 000 and

Table 1.8 Increased volatility of returns due to leverage

1	Return on project finance with	£200 of equity	15%
	Return	=	£30%
	RoE	=	30/200 = 15%
2	Finance with	£100 equity	
		£100 debt @ 10%	
		Return	£30
		Less interest	£10
			20
	RoE		20/100 = 20%
	But suppose the return falls in a bad year to		£15
	Interest still has to be paid		£10
			5
	RoE		5/100 = 5%
	Whereas if debt had not been introduced		
	RoE		15/200 = 7.5%

the market value of equity reflected in the net worth of the company is £5 000 000. At zero leverage, let us say there is no chance of bankruptcy. The NPV of the cost of bankruptcy is zero. At leverage levels of 20% debt, 80% equity, there is a 25% chance of bankruptcy. The expected NPV of bankruptcy costs is therefore £250 000, reducing the NPV of shareholders' wealth to £4 750 000. This reduced NPV will be reflected in a reduced share price, unless the increase in debt leads to increased returns that more than compensate for this increased 'cost' of bankruptcy. Nonetheless, there must come a time when the probability of bankruptcy is so great that the NPV of bankruptcy costs removes a large slice, or all, of the equity value.

Table 1.8 is a simple illustration of how risk, in terms of variability of returns to equity, is increased with leverage. If the company had remained unlevered then the range of RoE would be between 15% and 7.5%. Levered, it ranges between 20% and 5%. The increased risk will be reflected in an increased expected rate of return. After all, we all expect a greater return for a greater risk. If we look back at the illustration in Table 1.4, we see that, when the company is leveraged, the rate of RoE is raised to 16.8%. Suppose that, due to the increased risk introduced through leveraging, the rate of return required by shareholders was in fact 16.8%. To find the value of the shares, we would divide the NPV of the equity cash flows by the number of shares outstanding. The NPV is found by dividing the annual cash flow (with the simplifying assumption of no growth and in perpetuity) by the required rate of return, i.e. £420 000/0.168 = £2500 000 and 2 500 000/2 500 000 = £1.00 per share. In other words, although the absolute return, or EPS, has increased, the share value has remained the same. Therefore, to determine whether there has been an increase in shareholders' wealth, we need to determine the net effect on share price after making an adjustment for risk. The critical question, then, is whether the increase in EPS is exactly offset by an increase in the required rate of RoE. For this, we need some way of relating increased risk to increased rate of return and, for all its imperfections, the capital asset pricing model (CAPM) still remains a central theory for the pricing of risk.

The capital asset pricing model

When cash flows are discounted to give net present values, the 'correct' discount rate needs to be used. Too low a discount rate and projects that should be rejected will be accepted, and too high a discount rate, vice versa.

The discount rate should reflect the cost of capital to a company. The cost of capital is the weighted average of the various sources of finance available to a company. To keep life simple, let us say debt and equity. The cost of debt is reasonably easy to discover: ask a bank!

The cost of equity, or to put it another way, the rate of return required by a shareholder, is more difficult. A way is needed to find a risk-adjusted required rate of return for equity. It is obvious that a shareholder in a blue chip company will not expect as high a rate of return as an investor in, say, a new biotechnology company, given that the risk of the established blue chip is lower.

Markowitz (1952) noticed that the variability of returns on a portfolio of shares was lower than the variability of returns on individual shares, variability of returns being the way risk is measured. It was also noticed that risk could never be diversified away completely. This led to the splitting of risk into two parts, diversifiable and undiversifiable risk.

Diversifiable (sometimes referred to as unsystematic) risk is that risk which is particular to a company, e.g. a prospecting company may or may not find oil. If it does, the result is a bonanza, if it does not, doom and gloom as dollars disappear into the ground. However, if one invests in more than one prospecting company, say in ten, then if eight do not find anything, chances are two will, and this will provide an adequate rate of return over the whole portfolio.

Undiversifiable (sometimes referred to as systematic) risk relates to the way in which the whole market reacts to events, i.e. in economic recession, if oil prices drop, this will affect all the prospecting companies as well as all the other companies in the market. However, not all companies are affected to the same extent. Some react with more volatility to market falls and rises than others, e.g. when there was a coup in Russia, the whole market index fell, but not all shares fell to the same degree as the market index.

Now, how can this splitting of risk be utilised? First, markets tend to charge or expect a rate of return over and above the risk-free rate (Government security, no variation in return) in return for extra risk. Secondly, if diversifiable risk, or the individual risk pertaining to a company, may be diversified away, it ceases to be a risk and therefore will not be charged for. This leaves the undiversifiable risk or how that company's returns will vary in relation to variations in the whole market. This variability is measured over a number of years and is converted into a measure, beta, which essentially indicates how volatile an individual company's shares are compared with the market. (For information, beta = covariance of the stock in question and the market returns/variance of market returns.) This is used as a relative measure of risk. Over time, a number of studies have shown that the stock market should give a rate of return of about 7–8% over and above the risk-free rate. So, putting all these factors together gives us

expected market return = risk-free rate + 7 or 8%

To use this for an individual company:

1 Find beta. Best done by going to a service that does all the tedious calculation for us, say Co X beta = 1.2.
2 Find out the current risk-free rate, say 10%.
3 Find out current market returns, say 17%.

Then the expected return that a shareholder would want if they invested in this, slightly more risky than the market, Co X, would be:

$$ER_s = R_f + (ER_m - R_f)\beta$$

where ER_s is the expected (required) return on the sth asset, R_f is the risk-free rate (note no E or 'expected' term here, since it is known), ER_m is the expected return on the market, and β is asset beta.

expected return = risk-free rate + (market rate − risk-free rate) beta

or for Co X

$$10 + (17 - 10)1.2 = 18.4\%$$

or 7% premium for taking on the risk of being in the market

How would this now be used?

1 Deriving a discount rate for discounting cash flows on capital projects: let us say that the after-tax cost of debt is 14%, and the cost of equity is 18.4%. The intention is to finance the project with two-thirds debt, one-third equity, as with all previous projects.

Discount rate to use = marginal weighted average cost of capital

$$\left(14 \times \frac{66.66}{100}\right) + \left(18.4 \times \frac{33.33}{100}\right) = 9.3324 + 6.1327 = 15.465$$

So cash flows would be discounted using a 15.47% discount factor. If the NPV were greater than or equal to zero, the individuals concerned, debt and equity holders would receive their required return and so the project should be undertaken. If the NPV were below zero, the project should be rejected.

2 The equity required rate of return could be used to derive the current share price based on the future expected cash flows to equity holders by discounting all the dividend flows and any terminal value cash flow.

There are many arguments surrounding how valid the CAPM theory is, but it is not the purpose of this book to pursue them. Suffice it to say that the theory at least gives some measure of accuracy, and it is currently the best workable theory we have on which to base decisions. Accepting the CAPM approach then, what effect would increased leverage have on our company? We have seen earlier that increasing leverage increases the overall return to equity and debt holders. Focusing on the equity holder, this increased return should be reflected in an increased share price. However, if the current share price is a reflection of the net present value of the expected future cash flows to equity, discounted at the correct risk-adjusted rate of return, then the actual effect on the current share price will depend on whether or not the increased return is more than, or less than, commensurate with the increased risk.

Including financial risk

Suppose we have the following situation:

company A, with an unleveraged beta of 1.2
risk-free rate of 5%
expected market return 12%
tax rate 30%
profit before interest and tax (PBIT) £1428.57
profit after tax £1000.00
expected RoE = 5 + (12 − 5) 1.2 = 13.4
value of unlevered company is £1000/0.134 = £7462.65

Suppose again that the company decides to have 20% of its capital as debt, or £1492.54 worth of debt. The presence of debt will increase the risk of the company, and we are able to work out the effect on the company beta using the following equation.

$$\beta_j = \beta_{ju}\left[1 + \frac{D}{E}(1 - T_c)\right]$$

where β_j is levered beta, β_{ju} is unlevered beta, D is the amount of debt, E is the amount of equity, and T_c is the corporate tax rate.
So the new beta will equal

$$1.2\left[1+\frac{20}{80}(0.7)\right]=1.41$$

This will give a new expected RoE of

$$ER = 5 + (12 - 5)1.41 = 14.87\%$$

Now let us see what the net effect on the value of equity is when we use debt at a cost of 12%.

PBIT	1428.57
interest	179.10
profit before tax (PBT)	1249.47
tax @ 30%	374.84
net to equity	874.63

value of company to equity $\dfrac{874.63}{0.1487} = 5881.84$

However, if we take the original value of	7462.69
and deduct the value of debt	1492.54
the value of equity should equal	5970.15
so equity has fallen in value by	88.31

If we try the same exercise with an interest cost for debt of 5%, we find

PBIT	1428.57
interest	74.63
PBT	1353.94
tax	406.18
net to equity	947.76

value to equity at 14.87% $= \dfrac{947.76}{0.1487} = 6373.64$

or a benefit of 403.49

One could play around with tax rates and debt rates for a while but it seems that the level of the interest rate on borrowing will affect the net value of leverage to equity holders.

The implication of this result is that companies should carefully evaluate the effect on their share price of any borrowing. As long as the net expected return increases faster than the required return, then a degree of leverage is beneficial. This may have a further implication with regard to dividend policy where the payment of a cash dividend, based on a set of assumptions about shareholder required returns, leads to borrowing, which then changes the requirements.

Conclusion

In summary, we can say that in a perfect world the decision of how to finance the company, whether by debt or by equity, would not be a decision that would take up any of the financial manager's time. This leads us to focus on how the real world might diverge from the perfect world and, therefore, how the various imperfections might provide food for thought to financial managers.

Obvious imperfections such as transaction costs would impede the arbitrage process, as would the asymmetry of information held by different people. In addition, for many investors (though maybe not large institutions) individual leverage is not a perfect substitute for corporate leverage and, therefore, there is some value added in the company undertaking the leverage on behalf of investors. There are taxes, although not everyone pays them, and we have seen the effect of using debt and its tax advantage to increase EPS.

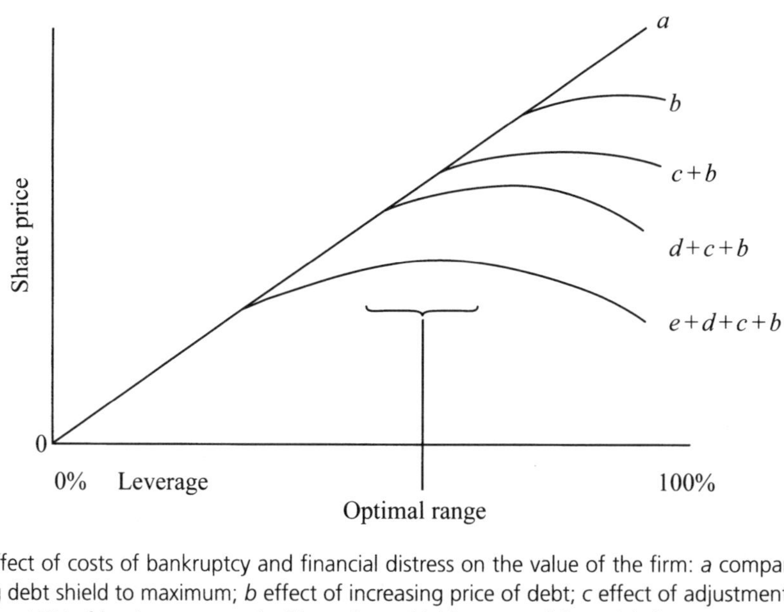

1.2 Effect of costs of bankruptcy and financial distress on the value of the firm: *a* company value utilising debt shield to maximum; *b* effect of increasing price of debt; c effect of adjustment for risk (including NPV of bankruptcy costs); *d* loss of tax shield; *e* cost of financial distress.

In spite of this, unlimited leverage is not the unmitigated good idea that it might seem to be at first glance. There are costs involved in bankruptcy, and therefore the increased risk of bankruptcy reduces the net present value of shareholders' wealth. There are also costs involved in financial distress, which reduce the value of the company. Eventually, companies will run out of taxable profits to shield with debt, so there is another limit to the amount of debt that it is worth taking on. As debt levels rise, the rate of return required by debt holders will also increase as they perceive that the risks that they are taking on begin to look like the same risks that the equity holders have.

Figure 1.2 summarises the effect of all these factors in a simple diagram. The net result of the various interplays would suggest that there is an optimum debt/equity ratio. In practice it would be difficult to pinpoint it exactly, and there is probably a range within which the company is able to operate without radically affecting share value. In the next chapter, since there are no magic formulae to guide the financial manager to the correct target area, the various approaches to setting a desired debt/equity ratio are discussed.

Lastly, it is worth pointing out that, for all the difficulties in handling risk, companies have to at least have a good shot at estimating what the correct risk-adjusted required rate of return is for shareholders so that correct investment and financing decisions can be made. It is the financial manager's job to minimise as far as possible the weighted average cost of capital in line with the company's activities.

References and further reading

Fama E 1980 'Agency Problems and the Theory of the Firm', *Journal of Political Economy*, **88** (April), 288–307.

Jensen M and Meckling W 1976 'Theory of the firm: managerial behaviour, agency costs and ownership structure', *Journal of Financial Economics*, **3** (October), 305–60.

Markowitz H 1952 'Portfolio selection', *Journal of Finance*, **7** (March), 77–91.

Modigliani F and Miller M 1969 'Reply to Heins and Sprenkle', *American Economic Review*, **59** (September), 592–5.

Financial textbooks

Brealey RA and Myers SC 1999 *Principles of Corporate Finance*, 6th edition, McGraw-Hill, Maidenhead.

Financial Times 1998 *Mastering Finance*, FT/Pitman Publishing, London.

Appendix 1.1

APPENDIX 1.1 Illustration of the equilibrium share price where no arbitrage is possible

	Company A	Company B
NOI	1 000 000	1 000 000
Interest on debt		330 000
Earnings to shareholders	1 000 000	1 000 000
Cost of equity	12.75	13.834
Market value of equity	7 843 137.2	4 843 137
Market value of debt	–	3 000 000
Total value of company	7 843 137.2	7 843 137.2
K_0	12.75	12.75
Investor in B		
1 Sell 2% of B	96 862.74	earnings 13 400
2 Borrow 2% of B's debt	60 000.00	
	156 862.74	
3 Invest in 2% of A	156 862.74	
Funds left over	0	the same
4 Earnings from A	20 000	
Interest cost	6 600	
	13 400	

Chapter 2 Setting optimum debt/equity ratios: theory and practice

Introduction

There are a number of different ways of approaching the issue of the balance between debt and equity financing. Financial managers who wish to stay employed will be relieved to notice that none of these approaches tells the company what the answer is, and so someone needs to make a decision. They all give some guidance, but leave the particular solution to managerial judgement as to what balance is actually correct for a particular company, given the company culture, expected economic environment and a multitude of other variables that will have some impact on future business prospects.

First, we shall look at some of the empirical evidence to see what common characteristics appear to play a part in determining what capital structure is optimum for a company or industry. The last section in this chapter examines whether there are international differences in capital structures.

Factors that influence capital share structure: the empirical evidence

There have been a number of studies concerning the factors that influence capital structure. In this section, we look at the following factors that have been 'uncovered' by research:

- industry norms;
- size of company;
- asset type;
- growth prospects of the company;

- volatility of earnings;
- profitability;
- non-debt tax shields.

Industry norms

The first issue to consider is whether there appear to be norms related to industry classification. For the US, the data are mixed. In a study of 12 unregulated industries, Scott (1977) drew the conclusion that '. . . the financial structure of firms in a given industry do cluster in a definite way' and also that firms identify an optimal capital structure for their industry. However, Ferri and Jones (1979) found only a slight relation between industry and capital structure, and Martin and Henderson (1984) found that only a few debt ratios exhibited significant differences between industries. Richard Castanias (1983) 'examined the relationship between failure rates and leverage ratios for 36 lines of business' and found that 'firms in lines of business that tend to have "high" failure rates also tend to have less debt in their structure'. His results also showed that firms do try to hold an optimum debt/equity ratio based on expected default costs, and this is inconsistent with the capital structure irrelevance argument of Miller (1977). For the UK, there are relatively few studies. A recent study by Varela and Limmack (1993) tested for differences in the capital structure ratios for 112 firms in nine industry groupings using data from 1967–86. They used six capital structure ratios including debt/assets, debt/equity and coverage ratios. They found that there were significant differences between the respective company's capital structures within industry groupings, suggesting that there was no optimal structure for an industry. Although they found that significant differences do exist between the nine industries considered, these were mainly attributable to the motor vehicles industry. Given these findings, it is difficult to support the notion of industry norms. However, in a study of the factors that explain differences across industries in leverage, Bennett and Donnelly (1993) found that industrial classification explained 18.1% of the variations in leverage, i.e. that there are industry norms.

While these results appear annoyingly contradictory, there may be rational explanations. It would not be surprising if there were similarities amongst companies within an industry, since they would be influenced by the same factors. Seasonality or sensitivity to the economic cycle would be common, as would, probably, the characteristics of the productive assets. However, differences would also be expected between companies due to differences in approach, culture and attitude to risk. A strategy of growth by acquisition may give rise to a different set of financial characteristics from those that result from a strategy of organic growth.

In addition, it may be difficult to find a large sample of companies that represent only one industry, since many large groups are diversified across industries. Nonetheless, if stock analysts are looking for particular ratio values, management should have a good story as to why their company is deviating from the norm. As mentioned above, it is possible that industries do show norms because of the underlying characteristics of the business.

Size

One might think that the larger the company the larger the debt burden that such a company could accommodate. This would be for a number of reasons. A large, well-diversified company should, through the portfolio effect, have a lower volatility of earnings and therefore lower risk and should, as a result, be able to support a higher proportion of debt. In addition, a large multinational company (MNC), as well as diversifying the markets for its products, will also have access to a larger range of capital markets throughout the world and will thus be able to lower its cost of debt. There are economies of scale in bankruptcy costs and in issuing securities. For all these reasons, we would expect higher debt levels with larger firms than with smaller firms. Bennett and Donnelly (1993) found just such a positive relationship in their study of company data for 1977–88 covering 433 companies in 19 industries. It is interesting to note that, in a study comparing domestic company (DC) leverage versus MNC leverage, Lee and Kwok (1988) found, contrary to the arguments used above, that MNCs had lower leverage than DCs even though they appeared to have lower bankruptcy costs than DCs. The reason may be that MNCs have higher agency costs due to additional factors such as political risk and international market imperfections. They also found that industrial differences explained a large number of the differences in capital structures between MNCs and DCs.

Another explanation for this apparent anomaly between DCs and MNCs may be found in Myers' 'pecking order theory' (Myers, 1984; Myers and Majluf, 1984). This theory puts forward the idea that managers will prefer to use the most readily available funds first and, when these are used up, they will go to the next cheapest and easiest source of funds. The pecking order will therefore be: retained earnings, debt and, finally, new issues of equity. If MNCs have higher profitability and higher retained earnings than DCs, this would explain their lower debt equity ratios. This effect may be reinforced in smaller companies, which, if fast growing, do not accumulate enough reserves to fund their growth and do not have ready access to the capital market, thus making bank debt the most cost-effective alternative. This will be reflected in higher short-term debt ratios and lower long-term debt ratios.

Asset type

It could be argued that an industry with a relatively high ratio of fixed assets in the balance sheet would suffer from a high operational risk. In other words, a high volume of sales would be needed to cover the fixed costs. Sales above the break-even point would be very profitable, while sales below the high fixed costs would reduce the profit quite dramatically. With this in mind, it would seem foolish for management to add a high financial risk to a high operational risk by leveraging up with debt. Therefore, we would expect to see a negative relationship between asset levels and debt levels.

Paul Marsh (1982) found that companies behave as if they have target debt levels in mind and that these levels are, amongst other things, a function of size. Marsh found not only that the larger the company the more likely it is to issue debt, but also that the higher the ratio of fixed assets to total assets the more likely the company is to issue debt. The reason for this may lie in Scott's (1977) hypothesis that the agency costs of secured debt are lower than those of unsecured debt. It would follow that companies with a high level of securable assets would have a high level of debt. Using plant and machinery divided by total assets as their proxy for securability, Bennett and Donnelly found that there was a significant and positive relationship between securability and debt levels. Presumably, some caution has to be exercised here, since plant and machinery can be very variable in terms of its alternative use values. A Boeing 747, for instance, can be used by another airline if the original owner (or lessee) goes bankrupt (ignoring issues such as the state of demand and useful life left). On the other hand, a plant built for a specific and 'one-off' purpose, e.g. some chemical process, has a very different value as a going concern versus its scrap value. Nonetheless, securability of assets does appear to be important. This can be usefully contrasted with companies such as high technology or pharmaceuticals, a large part of whose assets are intangible and which tend to operate with higher levels of equity.

Growth prospects

Myers (1984) propounded the theory that part of a company's current value, against which borrowing can be made, is derived from the present value of options to undertake investments in the future. If the debt matures after the time to decide to take up the investment opportunity has passed, then there is a chance that equity holders may decide that it makes economic sense not to make the investment and not to pay back the debt. For example, suppose there is an opportunity to develop a new product. Today it looks as if the present value of this opportunity is £1 000 000. The company borrows £700 000 against this. Now suppose that some time passes and the management needs to make the investment, say, of £300 000. If, now, the expected present value is still £1 000 000 or more, the management will invest, since £1 000 000 ≥ £700 000 (to be paid back) + £300 000 (the investment). If, however, it is less than £1 000 000, it makes more sense not to invest, and not to pay back the loan. This situation can lead to under-investment, as, even though the project has a positive net present value, the management will not invest in it since most of the benefit will go to the bond holders, not the equity holders. It is difficult to believe that managers take this opportunist approach all the time and, in a large multinational, it would be difficult to unbundle all the individual projects and analyse them and the overall funding patterns in this manner. However, in general a company does have a decision to make as to whether or not to keep trading when it looks at the broad picture of cash-flow-generating possibilities, use of equity and liability to pay debt.

The extract from *The Financial Times* reproduced below may well illustrate just such an option. In this case, the jump of 18p in the share price shows that the equity holders believe that this opportunity will benefit them as well as any debt holders, but what if Batman and Spiderman, riding high at the time, should have joined the Mutant Turtles in relative obscurity? If Myers' theory is correct, and if bondholders recognise this sort of behaviour, companies with a large part of their value represented by growth prospects might be expected to have lower gearing than average.

'Batman enters Bluebird nest' by Geoff Dyer

Batman and Spiderman are to join Mickey Mouse and Donald Duck on the miniature play-sets to be launched by Bluebird Toys later this year.

Shares in the UK toy group jumped 18p to 338p yesterday after Bluebird announced it had acquired the rights to use the two classic super-heroes.

Batman has been licensed to the group by DC Comics, part of Time Warner group, and is to be distributed outside the UK by Hasbro, the US toys group which has a 6 per cent stake in Bluebird.

Hasbro has also agreed to distribute the Spiderman product, which has been licensed by Toy Biz, part of the Marvel Entertainment group. Bluebird will distribute both products in the UK.

The deal follows a similar three-way agreement Bluebird signed in October with Disney and Mattel, which rivals Hasbro in the US for the top position in the toy market.

The collectable play-sets, which also feature Disney characters such as the Lion King and Pocahontas, are due to be launched in March.

Mr Chris Burgin, chief executive, said the deal extended the group's range and decreased its dependency on Mattel for distribution.

'It shows that a small company can deal with these giant US corporations,' Mr Burgin said.

Extract from *The Financial Times*, 23 January 1996

Using past growth rates as a proxy for future growth rates, Bennett and Donnelly found no support for Myers' hypothesis. They did point out that their proxy was not necessarily a very good one, as it was unable to distinguish between the value flowing from options to invest and the growth that is due to existing projects. Opler and Titman (1994) compared US companies that issued debt and equity between 1976 and 1993 to see whether they could derive any explanation for their behaviour. Their results suggested that 'both the static trade-off and the pecking order explanations of capital structure choice theories are useful in explaining firm behaviour'. They also found that distressed firms were less likely to issue equity where the main benefits would accrue to bondholders. Firms with high long-term leverage and current losses were more likely to issue debt.

Volatility of earnings

In bad years, companies do not have to pay out dividends and the average pay-out expected by shareholders over time may be maintained by higher than average pay-outs in good years. Thus, a company with highly volatile earnings is able to survive the booms and slumps of the earnings cycle. The same is not normally true of interest and principal payments due on a loan. An event of default can give rise to the recalling of the loan. Even if the lender did not do that, the threat of it may enable them to exact better terms (from their perspective!) in a renegotiation. A company with high earnings volatility would therefore have lower gearing than the average. In fact, Bennett and Donnelly found a positive relationship between earnings volatility and leverage. This surprising result may be explained with reference to the respective costs of bankruptcy and agency. Bradley *et al.* (1984) have shown that the costs of bankruptcy need to be quite significant before it has an effect. Nonetheless, it remains a slightly surprising result.

Profitability

If Myers is correct in his pecking order theory, companies with high profitability would have lower borrowing on average, since a greater part of any new investment could be made from internally generated funds. This would depend on the overall investment opportunities presented to the company, but, all things being equal, we would expect lower debt/equity ratios than for lower profitability companies. This is counter to the argument that says that greater profitability means greater debt service capacity, which would encourage more borrowing, not less.

Using operating income scaled by total assets as a proxy for profitability, Bennett and Donnelly found that there was an inverse relationship between profitability and the degree of leverage, which gives support to the Myers' pecking order theory.

Non-debt tax shields

Debt is not the only way to reduce tax. Capital allowances act as tax shields, as does expenditure on research and development and advertising. It is argued, therefore, that where a company has large non-debt tax shields (NDTS), the borrowing level will be lower, since the tax advantage of borrowing will not be so large or, where other NDTS take up all the tax, of no value at all. In those circumstances only that degree of borrowing which lowers the overall weighted average cost of capital through being 'cheaper' than equity and which is not counterbalanced by a *proportional* increase in the cost of equity, will be undertaken. Bennett and Donnelly use the potential deferred tax liability divided by total assets as their proxy for NDTS. If the hypothesis above (see DeAngelo and Masulis, 1980) is correct, there should be a negative relationship between the figures derived as above and debt levels, Bennett and Donnelly did in fact find a significant negative relationship.

Additional results

In the Bennett and Donnelly study, two other interesting results were obtained. Firstly, they found that the best results were obtained when market, as opposed to book, values of equity were used. Secondly, they often found that when short-term debt as well as long-term debt was included in the debt figures, this tended to reduce the significance of the figures. Indeed, with the exception of the result for profitability, all the results were significant when only long-term debt was used. This may indicate that short-term debt is used mainly for short-term adjustments until such time as the long-term ratio can be brought back into the range desired by management.

Practical implications

Industry norms

Dealing first with the issue of industry norms then on the basis that particular financing structures are appropriate for particular types of business because of the nature of the business cycle or the type of assets, some guidance may be taken from the ratios of other companies in the same industry. If the debt/equity ratios for an industry appear to be roughly the same, there is an assumption that this is a suitable mix for that industry. Unless the managers of those companies are all stupid, or the management of a company has discovered a way to manage the company that is totally unique, then using the industry average may be a useful start point. It must be remembered that stock analysts would be prompted to ask awkward questions if they found a ratio that was too out of line with industry norms. If management is able to provide valid and persuasive arguments as to why the ratio for their company diverges significantly from the industry norm, no harm will be done. If, on the other hand, they cannot, the stock analyst will be left with a large question mark as to management's competence and the long-run expectation for EPS growth. This argument applies equally to very conservative ratios, as analysts and shareholders are concerned to see that assets and earning power are not wasted.

Many of the other factors discussed above are related to profitability and current or future earnings flows, and it is worth mentioning two other measures that may form proxies for these. These are earnings before interest and taxes (EBIT)/earnings per share (EPS) analysis and coverage ratios.

EBIT/EPS analysis

EBIT/EPS analysis takes as its starting point the objective of maximising EPS and assuming a constant price/earnings (P/E) ratio, thus maximising share price. The analysis looks at the various EPS that can be obtained at various levels of EBIT under different financing alternatives.

Suppose, for instance, that a company is looking at a new project costing £5 000 000. Suppose further that it has two financing choices: all equity or all debt. Equity can be raised at £2.50 per share and debt costs 11%. The marginal corporate tax rate on the project is 30% and shares outstanding number 5 million. We need to find out at what level of EBIT either alternative gives us the same EPS. To do this, we need two points so that we can draw a graph. First, choose an EBIT at random, say £1 500 000 and calculate the EPS under each alternative (see Table 2.1).

The analysis in Table 2.1 gives us two points for Fig. 2.1: A for the all-equity alternative and B for the all-debt alternative. To draw the graph, we need two other points. These are easy to find. With regard to them both, it is the minimum EBIT necessary to finance that alternative. For equity, this is zero, point C, since no dividend has to be paid (although we may not like the consequences).

For debt, the minimum EBIT that the company must earn is £550 000, point D, i.e. the amount needed to cover the interest cost in order to service the debt. At this level of EBIT, EPS is zero, as there are no earnings left over for distribution to shareholders. We may now connect the points A–C

Table 2.1 EBIT/EPS calculation

	All equity	All debt
EBIT	2 500 000	2 500 000
Interest (@ 11%)		550 000
Earnings before taxes	2 500 000	1 950 000
Taxes @ 30%	750 000	585 000
Earnings after tax	1 750 000	1 365 000
Earnings available to equity	1 750 000	1 365 000
Number of shares outstanding (5 million existing + 2 million new issue)	7 000 000	5 000 000
EPS	0.25	0.273

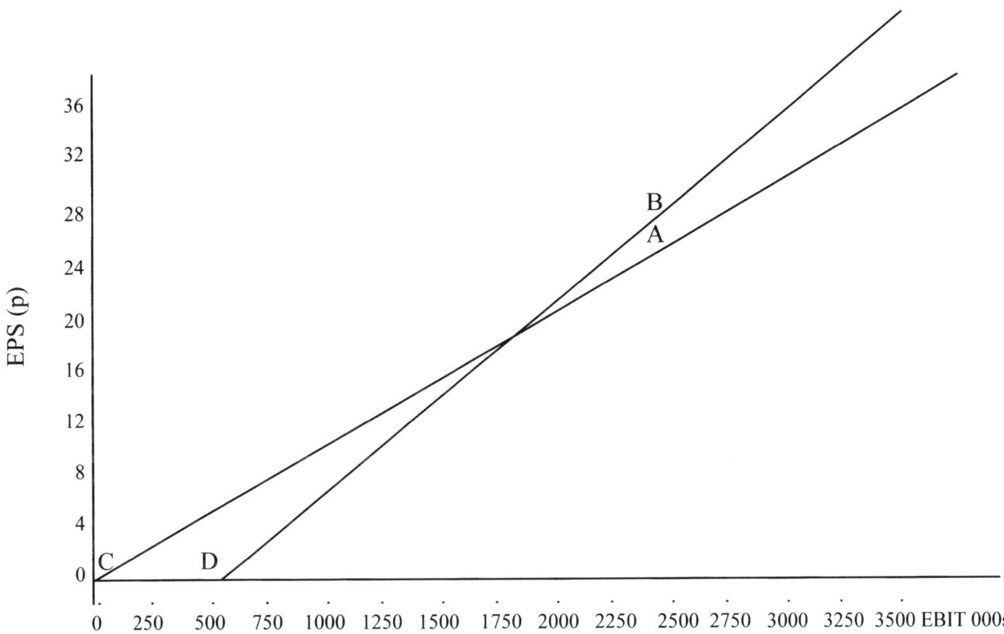

2.1 EBIT/EPS indifference point.

and B–D. Where the lines cross, either method of financing will give the same EPS. In the illustration above, this is an EPS of about 19p at an EBIT of £1 925 000. The fact that this may not be 100% accurate does not matter for two reasons. The first is that the figure derived is only telling you where you are indifferent, in terms of EPS, between all-debt and all-equity financing. We still have to decide whether we think our company results are likely to be above or below this number. Our estimate will itself involve a fair degree of inaccuracy.

The second reason is that we can in fact calculate the indifference point accurately using an equation:

$$\frac{(EBIT - C_1)(1 - T)}{S_1} = \frac{(EBIT - C_2)(1 - T)}{S_2}$$

where *EBIT* is the indifference point or EBIT, where EPS is the same, C_1 is the cost of alternative 1, C_2 is the cost of alternative 2, T is the corporate tax rate, and S_1, S_2 are the number of shares outstanding for each alternative. Table 2.2 shows the calculation.

It turns out that our estimate from the graph for the indifference EBIT was remarkably accurate. It can be seen that the problem with the mathematical approach, for any large company, is juggling with the number of noughts! Table 2.3 just proves that the EBIT gives us the same EPS under either financing alternative.

The company in question now needs to make a decision. If it firmly believes that under no circumstances, or at least with a very small probability, will EBIT fall below £1 925 500, then it will choose the debt route. If, on the other hand, there is a fair chance that EBIT will fall below £1 925 500, then either the all-equity or less-debt route might be chosen to reduce the impact on the reduction in EPS as the EBIT falls. Different financing mixes can, of course, also be tried out.

Apart from the problem of not knowing what the EBIT will be, this method has one or two other drawbacks. There is, for instance, no indication of what the actual share price will be under each financing choice. It assumes, implicitly, that the same P/E ratio will be applied whatever the

Table 2.2 Calculation of indifference point

All share		All debt
(EBIT – 0)(1 – 0.3)	=	(EBIT – 550 000)(1 – 0.3)
7 000 000		5 000 000
5 000 000 (EBIT – 0)(0.7)	=	7 000 000 (EBIT – 550 000)(0.7)
3 500 000 EBIT	=	4 900 000 EBIT – 2 695 000 000 000
EBIT	=	1 925 000

Table 2.3 Proving the indifference point

	All equity (£)	All debt (£)
EBIT	1 925 000	1 925 000
Interest @ 11%	–	550 000
EBIT	1 925 000	1 375 000
Tax	577 500	412 500
Earnings	1 347 500	962 500
Number of shares outstanding	7 000 000	5 000 000
EPS	£0.1925	£0.1925

leverage. Given the earlier discussion on risk, this may not be an accurate assumption. In its simple form, the analysis assumes the same cost of debt for each leveraging possibility, but the cost of debt may well change. However, these issues, once raised, can be taken into consideration, and the method does have the advantage of simplicity, and maximising EPS is certainly one target that financial managers do have.

Coverage ratios

We have noticed that one of the influences on the debt/equity decision is the increased risk that occurs as debt levels increase. Because of the increase in the variability of returns that occurs, there is a greater chance that interest payments may be missed or, indeed, that loan covenants may be broken, so that the company becomes in default and may be pushed into bankruptcy. With this in mind, the wise financial manager will want to ensure that, with a reasonable degree of certainty, any debt that is taken on will be serviced. For this reason, the financial manager will keep an eye on the relationship between the expected level of cash flow before interest and taxes and the interest burden taken on. This is known as the interest cover ratio. It is usually calculated as EBIT/interest on debt, or in our example 1925500/550000 = 3.5. Using cash flow in the numerator will give a more accurate figure for the actual liquidity position, but using EBIT is quick and gives a good feel for the levels involved.

However, this deals only with the interest portion of debt repayment, and (many would argue quite reasonably) creditors usually require repayment of principal as well. Principal repayments are made out of after-tax income so that the principal amount to be repaid has to be grossed up to show the pre-tax amount that needs to be earned to pay it. This is done by dividing the principal repayment amount by $1 - T$, when T is the corporate tax rate. In our example, therefore, if the principal of £5 000 000 is repayable in five equal annual amounts of £1 000 000 each, then £1 000 000/1 – 0.3 or £1 428 571.4 needs to be earned before tax such that EBIT of £1 428 571.4, less tax of £428 571.4, gives the £1 000 000 needed. This can be incorporated into the interest cover ratio above to give a debt service coverage (DSC) ratio:

$$DSC = EBIT/[\text{interest} + (\text{principal repayment}/1 - T)]$$

In our example therefore, the new coverage ratio becomes

$$\begin{aligned} 1925000/[550000 + (1000000/0.7)] &= 1925000/1978571.4 \\ &= 0.9729 \end{aligned}$$

It looks as if a 10-year loan might be a more viable proposition here (with a ratio of 1.5)!

As mentioned above, having worked out what the ratio is, the company still has to decide whether or not it is comfortable with such a ratio. A major factor will be the variability of cash flows. The more consistent the cash flows from year to year, the closer to 1 a company may go. The more variable the cash flows, the larger the coverage ratio should be. In addition, the company should make sure that it looks at coverage ratios under the worst expected conditions, rather than focus on current earnings, which may be in a high part of a cycle. Another factor will be the conservatism, or risk averseness, of the management. The more risk averse, the higher the rate would be set. Another factor that may give some guidance is the average industry ratio.

Analysts and rating agencies

This has already been touched on, but it would be a reasonable approach for financial managers to obtain a feel for the market comfort levels with different degrees of leverage. Chapter 7 deals with the rating agencies' approach in more detail.

The international dimension

Why might the financial managers of companies incorporated in any one country be interested in international comparisons of capital structures, apart, of course, from a simple desire for knowledge? Where the subsidiaries are to be consolidated, the decision as to the capital structure of the subsidiary becomes a balancing act between the competing pressures of a number of factors. If the subsidiary is capitalised with a larger proportion of debt than the parent, this will increase the overall debt ratio on the consolidated accounts. This effect will be small if the subsidiary is relatively small, but may need to be watched where, either individually or *en masse*, the subsidiaries form a significant portion of the consolidated balance sheet. More debt may be desirable in the subsidiary for tax or political risk reasons. On the other hand, too much debt may be politically and financially inexpedient because the Government concerned wishes to see more 'commitment' to the country, a good-citizen argument. Failure to do this could result in sanctions (buying bans, employee problems and so on) or financial consequences (thin capitalisation – see Chapter 5).

If all the subsidiary's financing needs are to be supplied by head office, the capital structure of the company may not matter from a credit point of view. If, however, it is to raise financing on its own merit, the local financial community would feel happier with a structure they are used to. At the least, this same argument might apply to local creditors. If local equity investors are involved, they too will have some view, presumably based on local norms, about the type of leverage levels they feel comfortable with. The newcomer should also bear in mind that the local norm, assuming there is one, has been arrived at within the context of local customs and culture and may also indicate something about tax and the return local investors expect.

As with previous studies, the evidence as to whether there are country norms as well as industry norms is a bit mixed, but Sekely and Collins (1988) took a look at whether there were cultural influences on international capital structures. They found that cultural differences did contribute to significant country differences between debt ratios of companies within the same industry. There is obviously a problem in defining precisely what is meant by cultural differences, and the study does not try to sort out which cultural elements exert the most influence. The sort of factors that might be considered are: social institutions, aesthetics, language, material culture and belief systems. Material culture includes the economic structure, technological capabilities, legal and tax systems.

Aggarwal and Baliga (1987) also came to the same conclusion about country differences in their study of capital structure in Latin America. They found significant differences between countries and industries among large Latin American companies and concluded that 'these variations in capital structure mean that multinational and diversified companies must take them into account when developing and setting policies regarding the capital structure, financing, evaluation and management of their subsidiaries'. After all, the norms for a country should reflect the local reality of financial and business risks, and international companies should look to these for clues as to the existence of risks, practices, customs and financial regulations with which they are not familiar.

Conclusion

Textbooks suggest that EBIT/EPS analysis, coverage and industry comparisons will be important factors in setting the overall debt/equity ratio, or range of ratios. Since it is the net after-tax return that shareholders are interested in, we might also wonder whether the shareholders' tax position enters into the consideration at all. The pecking order theory suggests that ease and convenience, coupled with transaction costs will also play a part.

When looking at multinationals the local conditions will influence the capital structure of subsidiaries, as will attitudes towards political risk and translation issues. As always, tax will play a part. The next two chapters are written by practitioners. Both are aware of the theories and some parts of their approach echo the more theoretically based chapters. However, while not claiming that they represent every financial manager's thinking or that their industrial background would be typical of all industries, nonetheless it is hoped that the reader will be interested by their reinforcement of what has been said but also will notice those areas that do not seem to concern them.

References and further reading

Aggarwal R and Baliga G 1987 'Capital structure among Latin American companies', *Managerial Finance*, **13**(1).

Bennett M and Donnelly R 1993 'The determinants of capital structure: some UK evidence', *British Accounting Review*, **25**, 43–59.

Bradley M et al. 1984 'On the existence of an optional capital structure theory and evidence', *Journal of Finance*, July, 857–78.

Castanias R 1983 'Bankruptcy risk and optional capital structure', *Journal of Finance*, December, 1617–35.

DeAngelo H and Masulis R 1980 'Optional capital structure under corporate and personal taxation', *Journal of Financial Economics*, **8**, March, 3–29.

Farrar S and Tucker J 1999 'Determinants of the marginal capital structure decision', Accounting and Finance Paper 2, ABS 1999:4, Anglia Business School, Anglia Polytechnic University.

Ferri M and Jones W 1979 'Determinants of capital structure: a new methodological approach', *Journal of Finance*, **34**, June, 631–44.

Marsh P 1982 'The choice between equity and debt: an empirical study', *Journal of Finance*, March, 121–44.

Martin L J and Henderson G V 1984 'Industry influence on financial structure: a matter of interpretation', *Review of Business and Economic Research*, **19**, 57–67.

Miller M H 1977 'Debt and taxes', *Journal of Finance*, **32**, May, 261–76.

Myers S 1984 'The capital structure puzzle', *Journal of Finance*, **39**, July, 575–92.

Myers S and Majluf N 1984 'Corporate financing and investment decisions when firms have information investors do not have', *Journal of Financial Economics*, June, 187–221.

Opler T and Titman S 1994 'The debt equity choice: an empirical analysis', topler@magnus.acs.ohio-state.edu

Scott D 1977 'Bankruptcy, secured debt and optional capital structure', *Journal of Finance*, December, 1–19.

Sekely S and Collins M 1988 'Cultural influences on international capital structure', *Journal of International Business Studies*, Spring, 87–100.

Varela O and Limmack R 1993 'Financial structure and industry classification in the United Kingdom 1967–1987', Discussion Paper, Series no. 93/06, Department of Accountancy and Finance, University of Stirling.

Chapter

3 Elements of a group's capital structure

Introduction

The theory behind the optimisation of an enterprise's capital structure and thus the minimisation of its cost of capital was explored in Chapter 1. Chapter 2 looked at the ways in which the management of a company might make the decision on how much debt and how much equity to have in the company's total capital. However, there is more than one form of debt and more than one form of equity. This means there has to be a decision made about what particular forms of debt or equity should be used to provide the company with a portfolio of instruments that will minimise the cost of debt or equity, but still provide the flexibility of financing that the company circumstances demand.

When designing an appropriate capital structure for any enterprise, the financial manager needs to take into account a number of factors, the most important of which are:

- the size and nature of the business;
- the cyclicality or otherwise thereof;
- its objectives;
- its attitude to risk;
- its current and anticipated future tax position;
- the expectations and requirements of its owners.

This chapter will review various options for financing the capital requirements of a company. These options make up a spectrum from pure senior debt at one extreme to ordinary shares at the other. Particular emphasis will be put on the way in which the different elements may be combined to create a capital structure that is appropriate to a particular enterprise, meeting its needs in a cost-effective manner. The two strands of the discussion, i.e. how much and what sort, will then be drawn together from a practitioner's viewpoint in Chapter 4 and extended to consider the additional complexities of capitalising a subsidiary overseas in Chapter 5.

Overview

The spectrum of instruments

It is generally accepted that well-secured senior debt holders provide the cheapest source of long-term financing. This is because they are the least exposed to risk from the failure of the business, while, at the other extreme, holders of ordinary shares are the most exposed and thus require the highest return. This difference is further exaggerated in after-tax terms by the fact that interest is generally tax deductible while dividends are not. The range of products between the two extremes seek to meet the business's need for finance at an acceptable cost by providing different groups of investors with packages offering different combinations of risk and reward tailored to meet their investment requirements. At the same time, the different combinations of financing are designed to meet the company's requirements in terms of risk (liquidity and interest rate), on/off balance sheet, impact on leverage and cost. It is through this segmentation of the risk spectrum and its combination with tax-effective structuring that the overall cost of financing an enterprise can be optimised.

Ascertaining an appropriate capital structure for an enterprise

It is essential in designing a capital structure for any enterprise that this is done in the context of the needs and aspirations of the business concerned. For instance, what would be a very comfortable level of leverage for a mature business in a non-cyclical industry may be highly imprudent for a high-growth business in a very cyclical industry. It is also important that the capital structure is not looked at in isolation, since there are implications for the business's ability to operate successfully in many different areas. For example, the balance sheet will be looked at to demonstrate credit worthiness in order to obtain credit from suppliers. The company must demonstrate its ability to trade for some time into the future so that customers have confidence that it will be able to meet its commitments to them (perception in this area being at least as important as reality). It must demonstrate its ability to retain the risks that are considered appropriate to retain. This could be the ability to self-insure in respect of regular small losses rather than swap additional premiums for claims with insurers, or the ability to maintain some exposure to movements in interest or exchange rates if the cost of removing them exceeds the anticipated benefits. All these issues must be taken into account.

It is essential that an enterprise retain at all times funds or available facilities to finance the whole of its anticipated cash needs together with a margin for safety. In determining this margin of safety, the relative cost of maintaining additional facilities needs to be compared with the benefits. The period for which this needs to be formally in place will differ according to the type of business and its ability to generate additional cash flow in the short term. This will depend on the lead times within the business; for instance a retail business requires a much shorter period to turn assets into cash than a very capital-intensive manufacturing business. In this consideration, it needs to be remembered that overdraft facilities are usually available only at a bank's discretion and can be reduced or removed at little or no notice. Also un-drawn committed facilities may not be available if they contain a clause requiring a company to confirm on each drawdown that there has been 'no material adverse change' in its financial position. Such clauses can mean facilities cease to be available at the very time they are most needed.

It should be remembered that the directors of listed companies are required to confirm in the annual report that they have the necessary finance available for at least 12 months. This is a part of the corporate governance requirements and all directors run the risk of personal liability should they allow a business to trade while insolvent (i.e. unable to pay its debts when due).

The instruments

The first task, then, is to analyse how much finance a business needs to enable it to meet its aspirations with a reasonable margin of safety, to cope with the unexpected and the fluctuations experienced throughout a business cycle. The next task is to analyse the different instruments available and to combine them in such a way as to minimise the full cost thereof to the business, consistent with the parameters previously established. By combining the different instruments in alternative ways, the various 'pinch points' can be mitigated. For instance, if the constraint at a particular point is the ability under certain circumstances to pay interest in cash, then it may, at a price, be possible to defer interest for a period. It will then be necessary to appraise the value gained from removing the constraint against the cost. It is also important in reviewing the different instruments potentially available to ensure that any 'knock-on' cost of their use is fully taken into account. One example would be giving security for a loan, which may reduce its cost but may deny the group access to other sources of, say, cost-effective short-term funding. Another example would be where the benefit of having a low cap set for an issue of 'auction rate securities' should be compared with the potential damage to the issuer's credit standing and access to other markets from a failed auction. Auction rate securities attempt to bridge a gap between a borrower's need for long-term finance and an investor's desire for short-term investments. While investors frequently 'roll over' maturing investments, they need to be able to obtain their funds back if they are required at the end of each period.

The auction rate security attempts to achieve this by giving current investors the ability to get out of their investment at par on any roll-over date, providing there are sufficient alternative investors willing to replace them. The process is organised by current and potential investors bidding a minimum rate at which they are willing to invest for a particular period. The rate to be received by all investors is then set at the lowest level where there is sufficient investor demand to take up all the available securities. Such instruments usually have maximum and minimum rates, which move with market rates and with the issuer's credit rating (e.g. for a 'single A' credit rating 80–120% of 3-month London Inter Bank Offered Rate (LIBOR)). If at any roll-over there are not sufficient investors willing to bid to take up all the available securities, then existing holders are forced to hold them for the next period at the maximum rate (e.g. 120% of 3-month LIBOR). There is obviously a balancing act to be performed here by the borrower in relation to the setting of the range.

It has already been mentioned that the spectrum of potential instruments is very wide reaching, from senior debt to ordinary shares, but also breaks down between the short and long term. Thankfully, however, given the availability of the vast array of derivative instruments, the decision on the appropriate mix of fixed and floating interest rates may at least be separated from the decision on the appropriate funding instrument. The appropriate mix of fixed and floating interest rate exposure is, however, an important part of the decision on capital structure. Even the most ideal mix of debt, equity and various intermediary elements can be made inappropriate by having the wrong mixture of fixed and floating interest rate exposure. For example, suppose you have a business which may generate substantial cash surpluses in years 3–7. In these circumstances, then not only would it be appropriate to consider having borrowings mature during that period, but it would also be essential that the business did not find itself in a position whereby it had more fixed interest commitments than net debt. If it allowed this to be the case, then it would be in the position of having its net financing cost rise as interest rates fell, because the interest cost on its borrowing would be fixed but its cash surplus would probably be earning floating rates of interest.

In deciding on the appropriate maturity of the instruments chosen to make up an enterprise's capital structure, consideration needs to be given to the time horizons implicit in the type of business concerned. An oil exploration company, for instance, may regard any obligations due within 5 years as very short-term because of the lead time involved in developing a field to the point where cash is generated by it. On the other hand, a service business may be able to reliably generate cash over a much shorter horizon, which means that it would view obligations of 5 years as long-term.

It is generally accepted that the longer the term of committed funds to a business, the higher the relative cost. This is because the investors require compensation for tying up their funds (the potential loss of ability to take up some other investment opportunity), as well as the greater risk that something could impair the business's ability to make repayment. It is therefore important that the maturity of instruments chosen is appropriate to the business needs. The taking on of 25-year debt when only 5-year funding is required will usually result in the payment by the business of an unnecessary premium.

Classes of debt

The different classes of debt are, in some respects, clearly differentiated, e.g. it is either secured or unsecured. However, in many respects it forms a continuum from providers who are most insulated from loss (i.e. the most senior) through the various layers to those with the least certainty of repayment (i.e. the most junior). Seniority of any such lender can, therefore, be seen to be a relative rather than an absolute description of their position.

Senior debt

What entails senior debt will vary by business but, in general, it can be described as being the source of funding least exposed to loss from failure of the business. In some cases, these lenders will have formal fixed and/or floating charges over the business' assets but, in many groups, senior debt would describe ordinary unsecured lenders.

The provider of senior debt will be sheltered from losses by a business's capital and the more junior creditors. They will wish to ensure that no other lender obtains a position better than theirs, so would expect a borrower to provide undertakings that they would not provide better security to another lender without extending the same benefit to an existing senior lender. It is important to realise, however, that a senior lender can find their position undermined in other less obvious ways than this. Typically, a group of companies may borrow the majority of their funds at the parent company level, where they may obtain the benefits of economies of scale and consistency. If, however, a loan was made by a third party to an operating subsidiary, that lender would be in a better position to recover their loan, were there to be a problem elsewhere in the group, than a lender to the parent. This is because all the liabilities of the subsidiary would have to be met before any funds were available on liquidation to the parent and thus its lenders. This 'structural subordination' is an issue that needs to be watched with care. While in smaller domestic groups it is often avoided by having each company in a group enter into cross guarantees of each other group member's liabilities, this is very cumbersome and often not possible or desirable once the group has overseas subsidiaries. The solution employed by many larger groups is to keep any third-party subsidiary borrowings at a deminimus level with all third-party borrowings in the parent or specialist finance companies, who then on-lend the funds to the subsidiaries as necessary. This helps ensure that all lenders remain *pari passu*.

The main types of senior debt would include:

- domestic bonds and bonds issued in the euro markets;
- medium-term notes;
- money market loans;
- commercial paper;
- acceptance credits;
- overdrafts.

Senior debt is not necessarily secured debt, indeed usually it is not. The title simply refers to obligations that are the most senior of a business's debt obligations. In the absence of formal security arrangements, senior debt usually ranks alongside the claims of ordinary unsecured creditors.

Junior debt

If the senior debt in some way ranks ahead of unsecured creditors, ranking behind it would be varying levels of less senior obligations, sometimes referred to as junior debt. This is not necessarily subordinated in comparison with ordinary unsecured creditors, but its claims sit behind those of the senior debt providers, who may, for instance, enjoy a fixed or floating charge over certain assets or benefit from particular guarantees.

Junior debt would therefore be more expensive than senior debt but, as it ranks alongside ordinary unsecured creditors, it does not prejudice the position of such ordinary unsecured creditors in the same way as giving a lender a fixed charge would. It can therefore form an important part of a capital structure when there are secured lenders and the business is reliant on obtaining normal unsecured trade credit.

Subordinated debt

The claims of subordinated debt holders usually rank behind those of ordinary creditors and thus provide some additional protection against loss for such ordinary creditors.

Subordinated debt is a very useful way of providing such additional protection while retaining tax deductibility of the funding cost. This, together with the ability for repayment when no longer needed, also makes subordinated loans a very useful tool for intra-group funding, especially across international boundaries.

Subordinated debt can be of a stated maturity, perpetual or repayable on the occurrence of certain events. Repayment, however, will usually only be allowed if the auditors certify that, after such repayment, the entity has positive net worth and/or certain other conditions are met. These conditions may be tailored to meet the specific needs of the situation, e.g. that, after repayment, a company would still comply with its banking covenants regarding gearing, tangible net worth, etc.

The provision of third-party subordinated debt is often found in highly leveraged situations and in debt issues that attract some form of equity participation, e.g. convertibles.

Convertible debt

Convertible debt is often used by companies who wish to retain the benefits of tax-deductible funding costs but, knowing they are likely to need additional equity funding in due course, are willing to give investors the right to convert their debt obligations into shares at a fixed price. This price is usually at a premium over the current market price. The right to purchase is given in exchange for a lower coupon.

The investors are willing to accept a lower coupon than they would receive on pure debt because of the conversion option. In their eyes, the investment is a route into the underlying equity at the conversion price. The investor therefore compares the coupon with the yield on the underlying shares, the direct purchase of which would be his/her alternative. The convertible also provides the investor with some downside protection: should the underlying shares not perform, at maturity of the convertible loan, the investor is entitled to his/her principal back. Thus, from the investor's perspective, it provides most of the upside benefits from share performance together with higher income in the early years and a lower-yielding debt investment if the shares do not gain in value by at least the initial conversion premium.

As investors view the convertible as an alternative route into the underlying equity, they will often be happy for the liability to be subordinated to ordinary creditors' claims for little or no cost.

Exchangeable securities

Exchangeable securities are similar in concept to convertible debt but, instead of being convertible into shares of the borrowing group, the investor has the right to exchange his/her debt security for other shares. For instance, the holder of a substantial number of shares in a listed company such as Reuters may issue a bond giving the holder the right to exchange the bond for Reuters shares at a premium to the current market price.

From the investor's perspective, this is an alternative route into the underlying shares with the benefit of a higher initial yield. For the issuer, it provides a lower-cost means of financing the investment, although they have given away to the investor the benefit of share price appreciation above the initial premium.

It is also sometimes possible to build into such securities an option for the issuer to pay the investor a cash amount equivalent to the excess of the underlying share market value over the exercise price rather than transferring the actual shares.

Classes of equity

Preference shares

At this point in the spectrum, we have crossed the magic line set by company law and utilised in the UK tax code, and thus, instead of being a liability of the company, the instrument becomes part of its equity capital. While this has important consequences from tax deductibility and legal repayability perspectives, in substance there could be very little difference between the risk, rewards and rights of a preference shareholder and the holder of deeply subordinated debt. The legal and tax distinctions can thus be used to tailor the attributes of a particular instrument to meet the issuers' and investors' requirements in a mutually beneficial manner.

A preference share forms part of a company's legal capital on which creditors can rely for protection against loss. The law therefore enshrines a creditor's right to expect this to be eroded (other than by way of losses) only in very controlled circumstances. Therefore, preference shares can only be repaid without the specific consent of the courts from the proceeds of a new issue of shares specifically made for the purpose or from profits otherwise available for distribution.

In terms of risk, a preference shareholder ranks behind all creditors of the company and thus receives nothing until secured, unsecured and subordinated obligations have been settled in full. Preference shareholders are, however, entitled to their full return before ordinary shareholders receive anything. Typically, dividends would not be allowed to be paid on the ordinary shares if there were any due but unpaid preference dividends. Preference shareholders also frequently become entitled to voting rights if their dividend becomes more than a certain level in arrears.

Rather than receive interest, a preference shareholder receives a dividend, which is paid only if there are available distributable profits and is accompanied by the relevant tax credit. It is possible to structure the exact terms of the preference shares to meet an issuer's and/or investor's particular needs. Preference shares can be convertible into ordinary shares, have periods in which no dividend is due, participate in particular streams or levels of profit and so on.

The flexibility of preference shares makes them very attractive for use in various tax-advantaged funding arrangements. At the simplest, a company without any taxable profits might prefer to pay a dividend and the associated tax credit, where they are available, to a bank, instead of interest on which it will receive no tax relief. This is because the bank would accept a lower coupon reflecting the non-taxable nature of dividends received (depending on the tax regime) in comparison with interest.

Example

	Company	Bank
Interest	(100)	100
Tax	–	(30)
After tax (cost)/benefit	(100)	70
Dividend	(90)	90
Tax	–	–
After tax (cost)/benefit	(90)	90
Net benefit over debt	10	20

Ordinary shares

The holders of ordinary shares are generally the ultimate bearers of the risks and rewards of ownership of a company. As such, they are entitled to the full amount of any surplus after all other liabilities have been settled, but naturally they are the first to bear any loss.

As the ordinary shareholders suffer the first pain from any loss, they traditionally require the highest anticipated reward and have the primary rights to appoint and direct the management of the business.

Combining potential instruments

When the amount of financing a business needs and the relevant time horizon for the funding have been ascertained, and the various alternatives reviewed, the key decisions are then related to how best to combine the various alternatives, the objective being to create a mixture that meets the business's needs with a suitable margin of safety at the lowest acceptable cost, taking into account all the relevant factors.

It is rare to have the luxury of designing the entire capital structure of a business from a plain sheet of paper, more normally what is already in place would be adapted. While what is already there may not be an ideal starting point, it may not be possible and/or cost effective to change certain elements. In this regard, it is particularly important to be aware of any tax consequences of the changes and any perception issues. Moving from subordinated debt to a form of equity finance would mean giving up tax deductibility of the interest and replacing it with a need to provide a return in the form of dividends and/or capital appreciation. Or returning excess capital to shareholders could make employees or long-term customers concerned about the long-term future of the business. As always, perceptions, as well as reality, need to be managed.

As the different components of the structure have differing costs, intuitively one might feel that the lowest overall cost would be obtained by having the smallest possible amount of each class of liability. The financial manager would start at ordinary shares and work down the cost structure to leave the maximum amount to be raised from the cheapest source. There are, however, various problems with this approach, the most fundamental of which is that the costs of the different categories of liabilities are interdependent but their relationship is not linear. For instance, a small increase in the amount of ordinary share capital might have a major effect on the cost of subordinated or unsecured debt in a highly geared business, but little effect on the cost of secured debt. Also there are substantial fixed costs (both monetary and in terms of restrictions on future flexibility) involved in having various types of instruments in issue and, thus, too many classes of instrument could mean additional costs through not being able to benefit from the economies of scale.

Again perceptions are very important and are ignored at one's peril. It is important, therefore, at an early stage to analyse who the potential viewers of the capital structure will be and what their needs are. If a group's capital structure is viewed as 'racy', even if it is intellectually optimal, the group will end up paying more than if its structure was viewed as appropriate.

It is also important to build into a capital structure the ability for it to adapt to a business's changing needs. In particular, it is important not to lock the company into something with no way out. An example might be issuing preference shares from the parent company of a group may be dangerous if they need to be redeemed, as the parent company's distributable reserves would be badly depleted. If, however, the preference shares had been issued by a subsidiary, with a suitably worded guarantee so they had the same rights, they could be redeemed from the proceeds of an intra-group subscription of shares into the issuing subsidiary.

Conclusion

It can be seen from this review of the potential elements that go to make up an enterprise's capital structure that there is no one right capital structure either in terms of the proportions of debt to equity or, within these two broad categories, the various types of debt or equity. It must be driven by the underlying needs of the business and is a matter of judgement where to set the various trade-offs between flexibility and certainty, short-term and long-term funding, downside protection and cost, cost of the instrument versus certainty and liquidity versus cost.

It is also essential that the capital structure, both of an overall group and internally between the different international members thereof, be kept under review and developed as the needs and aspirations of the group change over time. If this is not done, what was once close to the optimal structure could rapidly become less suited to the new needs.

Like all other elements of running a successful business, it is important that the capital structuring is done as efficiently and as practically as possible supporting the needs and aspirations of the business and in this way bring its full contribution to the overall business.

Case study: Parentco Group PLC – £80 million, 7% 10-year convertible bonds

Introduction

In the following case study, the name of the company involved has been disguised, but it is nonetheless a description of a transaction that actually took place and is described by one of the protagonists directly involved. Readers will notice that, while not all the issues mentioned in the main body of Chapter 3 are mentioned, a good few are. As this is a case study, it reflects only those issues that were considered important by the management of the company involved at that particular time. To some extent therefore, notice the factors that were not given prominence.

The company

Parentco PLC is the UK-based parent of an international group of companies. Its turnover was some £1.9 billion with operations in over 35 countries.

The geographical profile of the group's turnover by sales market was US 50%, Continental Europe 20%, UK 10%, Asia/Pacific region 11% and the rest of the world 9%.

Treasury risk management framework/financing plan

The group had significantly enhanced its treasury risk management framework over the past few years. The key elements of this framework were the treasury policies, planning and reporting structures. Within this, the key to treasury planning was the treasury operating plan (TOP). The TOP was developed from approved budget and strategic planning data to ensure that it was in line with the short- and medium-term commercial ambitions of the group.

It reviewed existing treasury policies and operating parameters and, in addition, made recommendations for changes where necessary. The TOP also incorporated the financing plan for the forthcoming year and was subject to review and approval by the Board.

Parentco stated in its last Annual Report that 'active measures are currently being taken to extend the debt maturity profile of the group'. These 'active measures' were detailed in the TOP as part of the financing plan. While various forms of financing were considered, the conclusion drawn, specifically regarding the medium-term fixed-rate interest instruments, was that the convertible bond market was a more effective borrowing instrument than straight long-term debt. Furthermore, a sterling bond was preferred to a US dollar denominated bond, even though over 50% of the group's revenues derived from the US. The reason for this was that, at the time, the group had sufficient US dollar denominated debt, and sterling denominated debt was preferred for balance sheet translation exposure management purposes (see Chapter 5 for further discussion of translation exposure).

Convertible bond

A convertible bond is a debt instrument, with a fixed coupon for a fixed term. The holder of the bond has the right to convert the bond into ordinary shares of the issuing company at any time at a price that is fixed at a premium over the share price at the date of the launch. The coupon on the bond is substantially lower than other forms of long-term financing, the difference reflecting to some extent the value of the equity options given to the convertible investors. The value of this option effectively reduces the cost of debt to the company until conversion. A convertible bond is an issue of securities for cash. The amount of any issue is restricted under the pre-emption rules; this limits the size of such an issue to 5% of the company's shares in issue within a 12-month period or 7.5% on a rolling 3-year basis.

An issue addressed in the financing plan was the overall cost of a convertible bond, given its equity element. As the cost of equity is substantially higher than the cost of debt, the present value of a convertible bond and the subsequent issue of shares if converted, would, particularly on an after-tax basis, be higher than normal forms of straight debt issues. While this is so, the company believed that the strategy for controlled growth that has been successfully adopted by Parentco made this less relevant for the following reasons.

- The Parentco Group had, at that time, a self-imposed maximum gearing level of 40% (net debt/equity). This gearing level was set after experiencing difficulties some four years ago in order to re-establish investor confidence while the group implemented its focused business strategy.

- If the growth achieved over the previous 3 years continued in line with the group's stated objectives, it was considered likely at some period during the following 10 years (the maturity of the bond) to require further equity. However, at the time it was considered as debt as this was then the 'worst case' scenario in the event that the bond would either not be converted or, indeed, be redeemed at par by the issuer after 5 years. Should the bond be converted into shares, this would have a double-edged benefit on gearing by reducing debt and increasing equity.
- The conversion of the bond into equity is issued at a premium (in this case 17.55% over the then market price), compared with a rights issue, which is issued at a discount and thus will not disadvantage existing shareholders to the same extent. Furthermore, conversion of the bonds into shares avoids subsequent new issue costs (e.g. underwriting and associated costs) on those shares.

Practical issues of negotiating and launching a convertible bond

Once the approval of the Board for the financing plan had been received, the key issues which had to be addressed were:

- selection of a lead manager and underwriting group;
- preparation of documentation;
- market conditions, pricing and the launch of the issue.

Selection of lead manager and underwriting group

The lead manager was appointed in view of its success in placing the previous convertible bond issue five years before and its continued position as the recognised leader in this field. To ensure that the existing shareholders' interests were protected, the brokers to Parentco, were involved throughout the discussions. The brokers and one other were appointed as co-lead managers; three of the group's core banks were appointed as co-managers.

Preparation of documentation

The key documentation in the issue of a convertible bond is the prospectus, which summarises the main terms and conditions of the bond and gives information on the issuing company and a summary of the subscription and sale agreement. Much of the documentation of a convertible bond is fairly well established and is completed relatively quickly. The details of these terms and conditions are formally incorporated into other, lengthier documentation known as (1) Trust Deed; (2) Subscription Agreement; and (3) Paying and Conversion Agreement.

1 Trust Deed

The Trust Deed covers the terms and conditions of the bond (which may be in either bearer or registered form). It will include covenants (if any), conversion rights of the bond holder into shares, interest on the bond, adjustments to the conversion price, redemption and purchase of bonds, undertakings given by the issuer and an 'events of default' clause.

There are, effectively, no financial covenants demanded by the convertible bond market other than a limited negative pledge clause. The conversion price was fixed at 298p but it may be adjusted (normally downwards) if, for example, a rights issue is made; these adjustments are to reflect the 'bonus' element of such issues. Normally, ordinary scrip dividends and shares issued through an approved employees' share option scheme are excluded from the adjustment provisions. (Following a subsequent rights issue, the conversion price was adjusted to 288p/share.)

The bond holders can convert into the ordinary share of Parentco at any time. However, given that the bond holder has a fixed coupon of 7% (which was twice Parentco's dividend yield at the time of issue), and a fixed conversion price at the time of 298p, there would seem to be little incentive for a bond holder to convert early in the life of the bond. The bonds tend to be converted into shares when the dividend yield on the ordinary shares exceeds the bond coupon per underlying share at the then conversion price. They might also be converted when the share price is significantly higher than the conversion price and the bond holder wants to lock in a capital gain. Furthermore, the issuer can effectively force conversion through its right to redeem the bonds at par at any time after 5 years; this redemption right provides a 'floor' for the investor.

2 Subscription agreement

This is the underwriting agreement between the company and the underwriters, confirming the level of fees payable. The total fee was 2.5% and was split between an underwriting commission of 0.5%, a management commission of 0.5% and a selling commission of 1.5%. The allocation of the underwriting of the bonds is driven by the issuer to be agreed with the lead manager. In Parentco's case, they wanted to achieve a balance between overseas and domestic bondholders. CSFB and Cazenove fulfilled this. The selling and distribution commission is allocated to those underwriters who actually distribute (sell) the bonds.

3 Paying and conversion agreement and registrar
This agreement covers the administration of the bonds from the payment of coupons to recording movements between bearer and registered bonds.

Market conditions, pricing and launch of the issue

Parentco had hoped to launch the convertible bond early during the year, but market conditions were not significantly favourable. In practical terms, this meant that they had sufficient time to ensure that all the documentation was finalised as far as possible. Conversely, the market for new issues was weak, yields were rising and they had to ensure that confidentiality was maintained. These market conditions continued until early July that year and were then followed by the 'holiday season'. Given that the company would announce its Interim Results in early September, it was decided to defer the project until the start of that month.

The market picked up slightly at the start of September. The documentation was updated and each day market conditions were closely analysed. Under these circumstances, the company agreed to launch the issue in the week commencing 12 September, having agreed the pricing and amount of the issue on the previous Friday (9 September). The sub-committee of the board, together with the lead manager and both co-leads agreed the pricing of a coupon at 7%, with a conversion premium between 15 and 18% for a term of 10 years. They had previously considered a term of 15 years with the bond being subordinated; however, each of these options would have increased the coupon and thus was rejected.

The markets themselves were volatile on Friday 9 September when the pricing meeting was held, so it was agreed not to launch on Monday 12 September, but to be prepared to act immediately if market conditions stabilised. Monday 12th opened with a 0.5% hike in UK base rates; paradoxically, this had the effect of stabilising the market. As Monday progressed, the consensus was that the markets were holding up well and that, as this was the case, the deal should be launched early on 13 September before being exposed to further economic data (e.g. from the US).

On Tuesday morning, the company confirmed the pricing and market conditions with CSFB and Cazenove and agreed to launch immediately. At that time, the indicated coupon of 7% was some 166 basis points below the equivalent 10-year UK Government Bond and substantially below that at which Parentco could launch a 10-year straight bond. The market's initial response to the bond issue and terms was favourable, with the bonds reaching a high of 101.25% shortly after pricing; the bonds were placed by mid-morning, with the issue being oversubscribed. Shortly thereafter, UK gilt and share prices fell sharply; by late afternoon the FTSE 100 index had fallen by 43 points and the 10-year gilt yields had risen by almost 0.25%. These events, naturally, had an adverse effect on the bond price.

A term sheet of the issue is summarised in Appendix 3.1.

Critical success factors

Parentco believed that the bond issue was extremely successful in that it was oversubscribed (issue amount increased from £75 million to £80 million) and the premium was 17.55%, the higher end of the 15–18% scale indicated initially. Furthermore, the 7% coupon was substantially below the coupon at which Parentco could launch a 10-year straight bond issue at that time. They also achieved their financing objective of extending the debt maturity profile of the group, while maintaining the internal treasury management parameters on the mix of fixed/floating interest rates. As important, however, was the fact that they had set and achieved a fair price for their bonds, which traded over par initially. Subsequently, the bonds traded below par in line with the general fall in the market. However, the premium on the bonds traded at or above the premium established at issue.

Conclusion

The background to the bond issue has been summarised, as well as discussing how it met the criteria of the financing plan at that time and the practical issues faced. The factors leading to the success of this financing were as follows.

- The bond issue was part of a clearly defined financing strategy to extend the debt maturity profile of the group at competitive rates.
- The strategy was approved by the board.
- The board was kept fully informed on the project's progress and of market conditions through its appointed sub-committee.
- Parentco had proven experts to handle the transaction in the form of lead managers and other advisers.
- The company had seized a market opportunity.

A convertible bond is a form of financing, which a treasurer should consider as part of the financing armoury, particularly for any successful, growing company.

Appendix 3.1: £80 million 10-year convertible bonds

Term sheet:

Amount:	£80 000 000 (increased from £75 000 000)
Term:	10 years (unless previously purchased, redeemed or converted)
Coupon:	7% payable semi-annually
Issue price:	100 (at par)
*Conversion price**:	298p (based on a share price of 253.5p)
Conversion premium:	17.55%
Conversion option:	bond holders can convert at any time from 7 November in year of issue
Call option:	after 5 years (at par)
Listing:	London
Negative pledge:	yes
Cross default:	yes
Financial covenants:	none

**Following the subsequent rights issue, the conversion price was adjusted to 288p/share*

Chapter 4 Developing a capital structure: practitioners' approaches

Introduction

In the absence of a formula to tell us how much equity and how much debt to use, we need to look at how companies do decide on appropriate capital structures. This will involve examining what objectives they have in mind when addressing capital structuring and what factors will influence their decision. The previous chapters have looked at the theoretical approaches to deciding on the debt/equity decision, what appears to be important from observations of behaviour and the broad issues involved in the types of debt or equity that might be included in the capital of a company. This chapter now draws those issues together and focuses on those factors which practitioners say are important. The case study at the end of this chapter, while focusing on a particular industry and a particular company at a specific point in time, nonetheless illustrates the points made in the main body of the chapter although it carries the usual caveat that a different solution might be sought in today's market.

Major factors for consideration

It seems that there are three major concerns for a financial manager when considering capital structure decisions:

- the ability to service and repay debt;
- liquidity and refinancing risk;
- maintaining a degree of flexibility.

These are, of course, interrelated.

Debt service

If a company is unable to pay interest on time and repay principal on the due dates it is technically insolvent and in the absence of understanding creditors, perhaps allowing refinancing, it may go bankrupt. The amount of debt and the rate of interest to be paid in relation to cash generated pre tax is obviously an important element here, and the interest coverage ratio is one way of setting a broad level of total debt at which, and given a level of forecasted cash flows, the company may adequately cover its interest payments.

However, also of great importance, is the ability to repay the principal and this makes the pattern of maturing debt also important. For this reason the maturity profile, i.e. what debt is maturing in which periods, needs to be managed with care. There is therefore a balance to be struck, not just between the amount of debt and equity, but also between short-, medium- and long-term debt. Within each of these periods, the mix of instruments must also be managed to give the best balance between low-interest cost, flexibility and refinancing risk.

These interrelationships will be discussed further in the next section on liquidity and refinancing, but at this stage it is obvious that the financial manager needs to have as clear a picture as possible of the future cash generative ability of the company in each future period associated with different levels of debt.

Liquidity/refinancing risk

In a market with an upward sloping yield curve, i.e. the longer the maturity of the debt, the higher the per annum rate, interest costs can be kept to a minimum by keeping the maximum possible amount of debt on a short-term basis. This seems nice and easy, so problem solved. However, there is a but. Suppose the financial manager finances all the company's debt using a seven day advance. This means that the company has the money for seven days and does not have to repay it until the end of the seven day period, but at the end of the seven days will either have to repay the full amount plus interest, or if unable to do that, roll it over. In other words refinance.

What if the bank (or banks) is unwilling to allow the company to refinance? Lack of liquidity will cause the company to go bankrupt.

It is perhaps worth stating at this stage that being profitable is in itself not enough. There is a distinction between profitability and liquidity. Figure 4.1 illustrates the cash cycle in a simple fashion.

Now suppose a company buys raw materials for £80, adds a further £80 of labour and other costs and puts the goods into stock valued at £160. The goods are then sold for £320. The first question is, what is the profit? Most

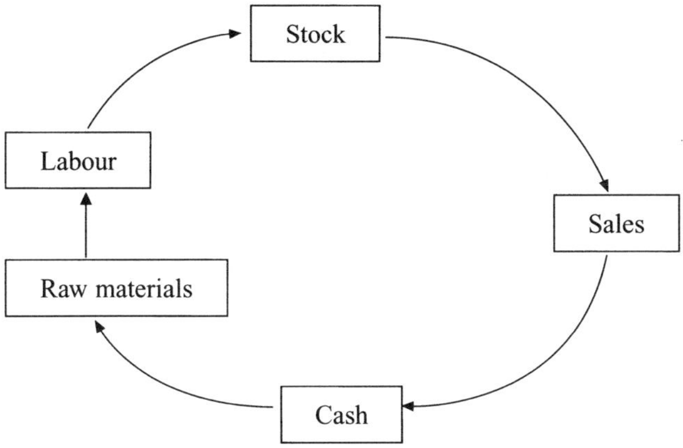

4.1 The cash cycle.

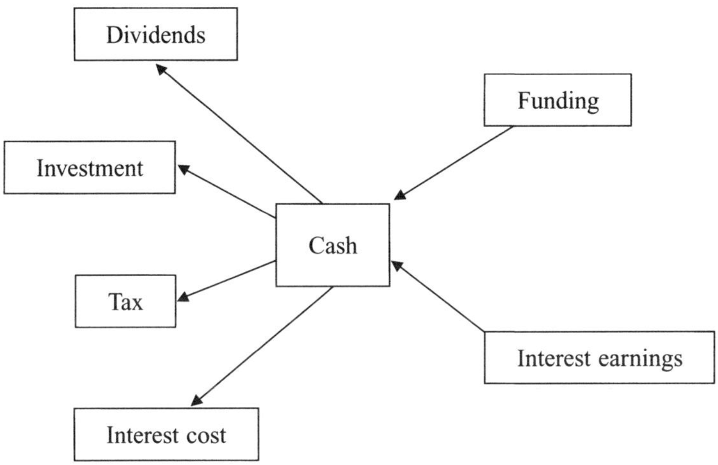

4.2 Cash items.

people would agree it was £160, i.e. sale of £320 less costs of £160. The next question is, what is the cash balance? Well assuming it started at zero then it could be anything between plus £320 to minus £160. Why? Well if the company has not paid cash for its raw materials or labour but was paid for the sales, this would give a balance of plus £320. If, on the other hand, it has not been paid for the sale (credit terms 30 days perhaps) but has paid for the raw materials and labour, then the balance will be minus £160. It is obvious which position is preferable and it is the aim of the company to be as cash generative as possible, as well as being profitable.

We can now fill in a few more items on the cash box of the cycle (but still keeping it simple) to give Fig. 4.2. If the company is minus £160 then it will need a cash injection to pay its suppliers. If it is plus £320 then it will use some of that for paying suppliers and labour, and use the balance for investment. The critical question for the finance manager is: will the company be able to obtain the finance?

An obvious way around this would be to borrow for longer periods and thus remove the liquidity problem to a future date. However, there are still problems with this. The first is that, unless the financial manager has a range of maturities there will be a large refinancing problem at some future date. While there may be more time to prepare for it, nonetheless, to have to refinance the whole of a company debt requirement and all that entails in terms of negotiations with banks, managing the process and not giving too much away in desperation, is worth avoiding by good maturity planning.

The second problem relates to cost and availability. A company may seek committed lines from its bank that it is able to draw down, or repay, under set conditions. This additional flexibility again sounds as if it has solved the problem, but there will be costs attached.

These could be obvious, i.e. a direct commitment fee is charged by the bank, or less obvious in terms of a higher cost of borrowing. If a commitment fee is charged and the loan is not needed, the commitment fee will still have to be paid, which could have a major effect on the overall cost of funds. The fee is charged because a bank will have to allocate a portion of its balance sheet to the company, whether the loan is used or not. This will block the bank's ability to utilise it elsewhere.

Furthermore, the ability to draw down a committed facility may be constrained by the existence of covenants, such as a 'material adverse change' clause. If it is one that operates in terms of the bank's judgement of such an event, then the commitment may effectively be almost worthless. As one treasurer commented, 'There is no point in entering into an agreement designed to act as a liquidity reservoir if it cannot be relied upon to be there when most needed. This right might lead a company to wonder whether it should be asked to pay a fee for such a commitment and whether it should itself regard this facility as short term in nature'.

The third problem is if all the debt is fixed for a long time. While this has the benefit that the bank (in absence of breach of covenant or other events of default) cannot demand the money back, neither can the company pay it back without penalty should it find it does not need it. In other words the company loses flexibility in how it manages its debt levels.

Flexibility

The financial manager needs to retain flexibility in three areas. The first is the total debt that is outstanding at any one time. It is not good from a company's point of view if it has borrowed at 10% for ten years, only to find out after two years that is has large excess cash balances which will only earn interest at 5%.

The second is in the instruments which the company uses. As markets change, tax rates change and indeed the company changes so the type of borrowing that a company may want to undertake will change, i.e. more or less equity or equity featured debt, more or less trade finance and so on.

The third area of flexibility relates to the interest basis of the debt, broadly, fixed or floating. While it is true that floating rate can be fixed with derivatives and fixed can be turned into floating these do have costs attached and it is the ability to move swiftly when required that is important.

In summary, the finance manager needs flexibility to:

- raise new funds in appropriate ways for new investments;
- repay unwanted debt to avoid wasting resources;
- take advantage of, or receive protection from, interest rate movements.

Forecasting

Most financing decisions are taken when there is already a balance sheet in existence to act as a starting point and it is rare to have the 'luxury' of a clean slate to write on. Either way the financial manager must have a view as to the future, as well as the present, when making capital structure decisions.

All businesses should have some form of forecasting. The method will normally vary depending on the time period involved and what the forecast is trying to attain. Very short-term forecasts for managing liquidity will be needed giving expected cash inflows, outflows and net balances on a daily, weekly, monthly, semi-annual or annual basis depending on the nature of the industry and how finances are managed.

These will be based on actual expected cash movements. Accuracy will be greatest in the short term, but in some industries even the next week can be difficult to predict. Forecasts for longer than one year may be based on broader predictions as to the expected shape of the balance sheet.

This will take account of future expected debt repayment, new investments and broad expectations of profitability. As balance sheets should balance, at the end of the exercise any lack of balance between assets and liabilities will indicate a need for financing, or repayment. It is obvious that the further out the forecast, the less accurate it is and the greater it becomes a hostage to fortune. Nonetheless some effort to plan and prepare has to be made since it would be a disaster for future sales growth to be constrained through a lack of financial resources to fuel the expansion.

The object with long-term forecasting is to set the broad parameters of future needs. As time progresses a refining process takes place which means that the proportions of debt and equity are adjusted and that within each category more definition is added as to the type of debt/equity, e.g. how much short-, medium- or long-term debt and how much on overdraft, fixed period advances and so on. This may sound a rough and ready way to plan for the future but its purpose is not to produce a perfect plan but to create an overall framework which allows for adjustment. After all, as one wit put it, planning is what you do while the world goes by. As an aside, there is a danger that once an item appears in the budget, say £5 million for a future expected acquisition, it is taken as approved and therefore to be spent without further analysis.

The broad issues

Transaction size and cost

What are the main attractions of debt over equity? Tax deductibility of interest has been discussed before, but there are other factors. Transaction size is another feature that needs consideration. Equity tends to be raised in relatively large tranches with a relatively narrow range between minimum and maximum tranche size. Debt on the other hand has a much wider range of transaction sizes ranging between the bite size chunks within an overdraft facility, through the larger loan deals with syndications to extremely large bond deals.

Transaction costs also vary and can be very low for debt, with no fees for uncommitted lines. Even after the various fees are added (e.g. commitment fees, underwriting fees, management fees) debt can still be a cheaper way to raise money than equity.

Flexible drawdown

Debt also allows a fair degree of flexibility, ranging from the total flexibility to draw down and payback associated with overdrafts, to the bullet repayment of a zero coupon bond. It is more difficult to reverse equity issues, which usually involves the setting up of share repurchase programmes. Speed can sometimes be critical to the successful completion of a deal and here again debt tends to have an advantage over equity, especially where an equity issue will infringe existing shareholder preemption rights. All these factors make debt look attractive. So why bother with equity?

Well, as discussed earlier the benefits of debt can run out. Tax deductibility of interest depends on having tax to pay. We have also seen that the level of debt will also affect the level of shareholder returns and the level of returns that shareholders expect. These considerations set limits to the amount of debt that a company may raise.

It is also wise to leave some leeway for further borrowing so that unexpected disasters as well as opportunities may be dealt with. There is therefore a limit to the amount of borrowing which it is sensible to do, which is set by internal forces as well as external forces.

Gearing measures

The gearing ratio has already been discussed but there are other dimensions which need to be considered in using this measure. Normally balance sheet values of debt and equity are used but these do not necessarily reflect the true values. Accounting policies will affect the level of balance sheet items but they do not necessarily reflect the true position. Take for example the value of equity. The net worth of a company in balance sheet terms is that amount left over when all the non-equity liabilities have been subtracted from the assets. This may suffice in those industries that are heavily fixed asset based but what about those industries where the assets may only reside in intellectual property rights, for example pharmaceuticals or software companies? Similarly, do the levels of borrowing stated in the balance sheet give the full picture? What liabilities are carried 'off balance sheet' which nonetheless give rise to fixed payment obligations and which should therefore be included in any debt service? It may be better therefore to use market values of equity in the gearing calculation (and certainly in any covenants relating to gearing) and all fixed obligations in the coverage ratio. It is worth remembering that the value of ratios is not in the absolute number produced but in how it is moving over time and how it compares with other companies in the same industry. If the basis for these comparisons is not the same and varies over time, the validity of using these ratios for guidance is called into question and the attraction of their simplicity in use should not seduce the user into over reliance. This is not to say that they do not have some power when the user is aware of these issues. After all, if a company, using equivalent measures looks to have twice the level of gearing of another company, then some interesting questions could be asked, and indeed conclusions drawn, about the contrasting ways the businesses are being run.

The industry

The industry a company operates in, or mainly operates in, will exert a powerful influence over the financing decision. A major consideration will be the degree of business risk that is inherent in the underlying business. Is it for example cyclical or heavily dependent on a particular technology or the weather? This level of risk is outside the control, to a large extent, of the management and is a function of their, and the shareholders', choice to be in that industry. We have seen that a wise use of gearing may enhance shareholders' return, but we also know that this also increases risk. Care must be taken to ensure therefore that while increased returns will be welcome, more than proportionate losses in the event of a downturn will not occur.

Since financial risk is an element that is under management control, the management of a company that already exhibits a reasonable, or high, degree of business risk, must be careful not to over-egg the pudding or they will be savaged by the shareholders. For this reason companies that are in industries with a high degree of earnings volatility will tend to have lower gearing.

Asset base

High fixed asset values, especially if they are easily identifiable and are able to be used by other companies in the same industry or other industries, can be used to secure debt and thus support levels of debt higher than industries without these characteristics.

The more marketable the assets and the longer their life, the longer the debt maturities that may be supported by them. Property investment companies exhibit these characteristics and so are able to find supplies of secured long term debt.

Outside influences

The perception that the markets have of a company has an impact on the company's ability to raise finance, debt or equity, in the market. A company usually has a history and the market perceptions have been based upon that history. Any attempt to radically change the character of a company, either in industry terms, i.e. moving away from the expected norms for that industry or from its own historic structure, will precipitate a lot of concerned questioning and requests for justification.

These requests will come in the main from rating agencies and equity analysts (perhaps proxies for the major institutional investors). Each looks at the issues from a different angle and this does not make life easy for the financial manager. Rating agencies look at a company from the perspective of the suppliers of debt and naturally their main concern is the company's creditworthiness. The analysts on the other hand, while wishing to see sound finances, have a strong focus on the company's ability to maximise shareholders' wealth. The financial manager needs to balance their two views so that each remains happy with the expected outcome. New debt must not cause a reduction in the rating, at least not more than anticipated, and must nonetheless be seen as revenue enhancing by the analysts. Creating and managing this happy balance is as much art as science and, as well as a knowledge of the instruments, demands a knowledge of the current markets.

Access to markets

We have looked at company and industry issues and taken note that factors both present and future must be considered as we plan how we want to structure our financing. Many of these issues are not influenced by the finance function but there are three areas which are: communication, the price to pay, and diversifying the supplier base, and these must be attended to if the company wants to be sure that it is able to access the markets as and when it needs to.

Communication

Would you hand money over to someone merely because they ask for it without telling you either what they are going to do with it or how they are doing with your money? Presumably the answer is no and the market is really no different. Investors like to be treated properly and this involves not just the maintaining of the promised flows of dividends and capital appreciation but also information about how the company will maintain this performance in the future. This information will contain as much detail as is possible so as to inform the shareholders and meet new guidelines on disclosure but not give useful detail away to competitors. Balancing these conflicting information needs is a clever trick in itself, but investors need to know just what they are investing in. They also need to know what a company's policies are on risk management. After all it is no good to investors if they invest in a company which is heavily exposed to the US dollar, or Japanese yen, specifically to take advantage of a hoped for strengthening of those currencies against their own if the company hedges the flows.

Keeping the investors fully informed keeps them happy in the good times and happier, or more forgiving, in the bad times. It is an old saying, but true, that bankers do not like surprises.

The price to pay

A good bargain leaves both parties to it feeling that they have gained and it is sometimes more astute to leave something on the table with an eye to the future than to be 'macho' and negotiate the last penny out of a deal. After all, in a market awash with liquidity the borrower may have the upper hand but these markets have a habit of turning around.

In the privatisation process, giving part of the service industries concerned away to the investor encouraged investors to subscribe to the subsequent privatisation issues. This had the effect of widening the investor base of shareholders in the country at large and therefore increasing demand. The bond markets operate in much the same way. A successful bond issue will see the spread tighten by a few basis points, i.e. the original investors could have charged less, while an unsuccessful deal will see the spread widen. The few basis points movement will be insignificant in terms of effect on the total financing cost, especially after tax, but psychologically will leave the market feeling slightly cheated or slightly self-satisfied and it will remember the good or bad feeling the next time around.

Diversifying the supplier base

A reason often put forward for a particular deal when analysed later is that it allowed a company to tap into a new source of funds. This could be a new market, say Tokyo instead of London, or a new instrument, say commercial paper instead of bank advances. This, it is argued, broadens the investor base exposing the company to new investors who have 'an appetite' for that particular risk. This is probably true and is often put forward as a reason why multinational companies, with easier access to overseas markets, have lower costs of capital than their equivalent domestic or smaller sized brethren.

After all it does make intuitive sense. Investors, be they private, large institutions or banks will have limits on the exposure they are willing, or allowed by the regulatory authorities, to take on. So once an investor has, say, 10% of its portfolio invested in one company it will need an inducement, hence higher cost to borrow, to go above this. At this stage it will pay the company to widen its supply base and head off for a new market where investors are looking for new investments.

However, as with so many things, there is a limit to the value in doing this. A wider investor base means more costs in terms of communication. The more widely spread the investor base is for any given level of debt, the lower the individual commitment to the company. For these reasons there is a balance to be struck between depth and width and many treasurers believe that 'deep markets and relationships represent far better long-term value so far as financial flexibility is concerned'.

For example HMC, featured in the next case study, when faced with raising £2 billion nonetheless concentrated on just two core markets.

Cash effects

It is tempting to think of cash surpluses as being a very good thing. So it is for liquidity purposes but as with the other aspects of finance, it is important to strike the right balance. Substantial cash balances have the effect of de-gearing the company, even when not used to repay debt. The return on cash, as discussed earlier, is less than when invested in the productive assets of the company and some analysts subtract cash from debt to produce gearing ratios. This underlines the importance of the longer term cash flow forecast based on the strategic plans of the company since the sale of a subsidiary, or part of a business, could lead to unutilised, large, cash surpluses.

Another problem with cash is the associated pressure to spend it. If it is spent wisely then no harm is done, but if it leads to paying large premiums for acquisitions and a lack of adequate financial analysis then shareholder value will be destroyed. There are good modern examples of this effect, witness the lending to the housing market in the late 1980s. Perhaps one of the best examples is from the late 1960s–early 1970s and the pressure on the international banks to recycle the huge balances of petro dollars leading to ill advised country lending.

Conclusion

In finance you 'pay your money and take your choice'. A financial manager has to balance all the conflicting issues and come out with the best mix available at that time and given market conditions. Figure 4.3 illustrates the 'push-me-pull-you' nature of this balance, while not intended to be a checklist of all the issues. As conditions change, so will the balance. These conditions include:

- interest rate levels;
- tax rates;
- reporting requirements;
- new instruments appear;
- world economy shifts gear.

It is therefore a moving picture and what a financial manager does in one year he or she would not necessarily do a year later. Indeed a different person looking at the same issues would probably come up with a different solution. The major considerations that need to be brought into play though do not really change, only the answers.

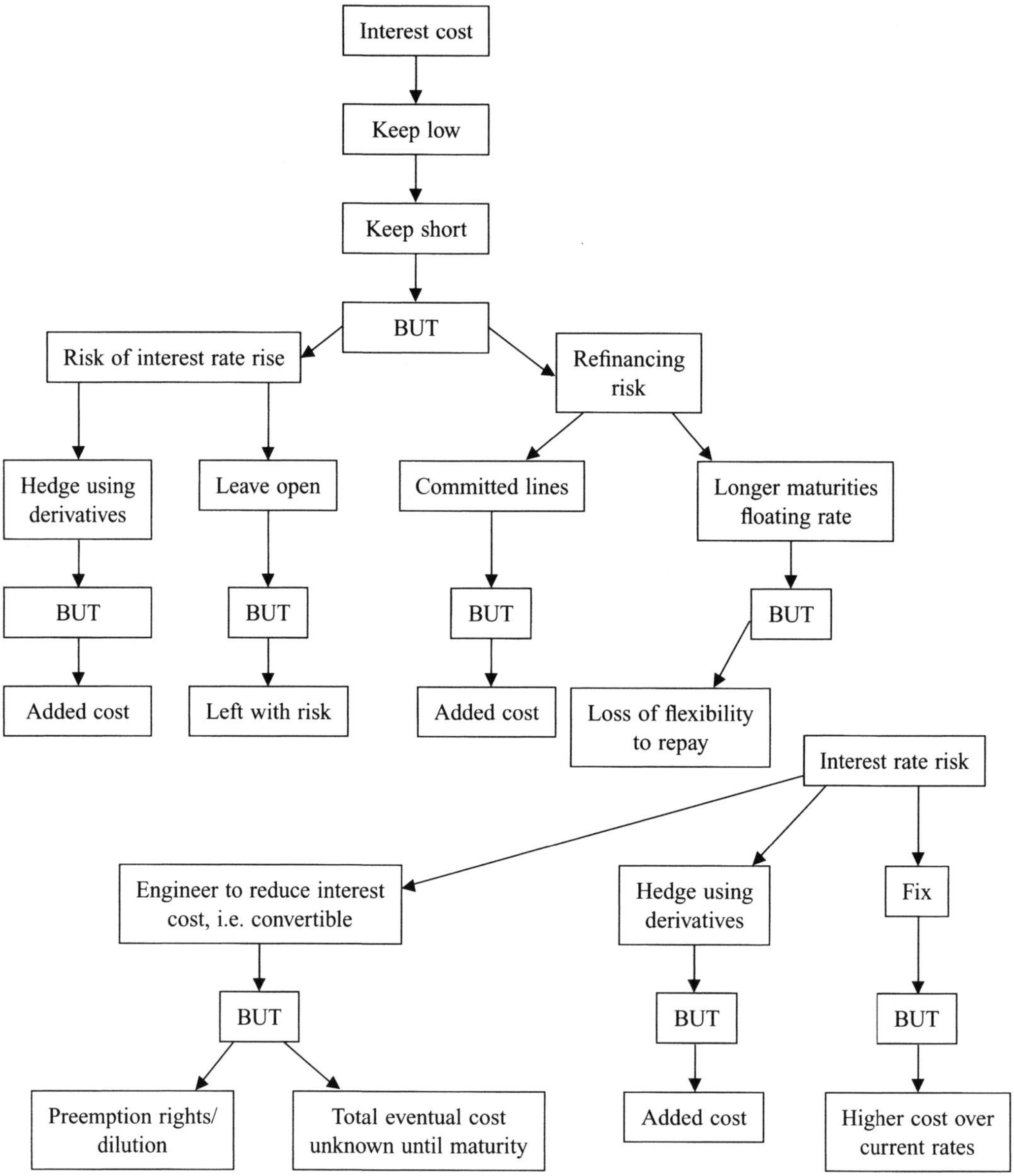

4.3 The interrelationship between debt service, liquidity risk and flexibility assuming an upward sloping yield curve.

Case study: Household Mortgage Corporation

Background

Household Mortgage Corporation (HMC) was arguably the most successful of the new breed of mortgage lenders to emerge in the UK in the mid-1980s. Following the breakdown of the building society cartel, which had previously set both mortgage and retail deposit rates, an opportunity arose for wholesale funded institutions to compete in the residential mortgage market.

The key to their competitiveness, and the reason that they were able to grow so rapidly, was efficiency. Operating efficiency arose from using intermediaries, typically from insurance companies, to originate their mortgages. A centralised processing and administrative unit was used rather than a network of branches, which gave efficiencies in terms of bricks and mortar. Last but not least, the company was also capitalised efficiently through leveraging its assets by issuing mortgage-backed securities (MBS).

The idea for HMC came from discussions amongst two or three city institutions who had observed the American experience of a huge and actively traded MBS market. They saw no reason why a market along similar lines should not evolve in the UK and were keen to accelerate its development by forming a company which would both provide the raw material for MBS issuance and also trade the securities themselves. The founders' intentions, bearing in mind their financial trading backgrounds, were that HMC would primarily be an MBS trader with the mortgage business, if not quite peripheral, definitely not centre stage. As we shall see, things did not go exactly to plan; but first the initial equity capital had to be raised.

Equity raising

In order to generate the economies of scale which would be crucial to HMC's success, the company would need to be able to support a mortgage portfolio of several hundreds of millions of pounds. It would consequently need a substantial capital base, and by the time the equity raising drew to an end in early 1986, HMC had attracted the largest amount of venture capital ever raised for an unlisted start-up business.

The initial equity target was £25 million. This amount was determined by considering the volume of mortgage loans that HMC would need to finance in the banking market prior to securitisation (the warehouse) and the gearing ratio that was expected to be required by the providers of such finance. It was also anticipated that, as in the United States, loans could be securitised capital free, i.e. any capital required as part of an MBS issue could be generated by selling the securities at a premium. It was thought likely that the banking markets would require a 20:1 ratio and that it might be necessary to warehouse up to £500 million of loans. Hence the initial objective of raising £25 million of equity.

There was in fact an active debate among prospective shareholders about the maximum level of gearing that HMC should be permitted. The debate suggested that certain of the shareholders did not quite appreciate the nature of the finance company in which they were about to invest. Those shareholders with some experience of securitisation in the United States wanted no gearing restriction, whilst others were adamant that 20:1 (including securitised assets) was to be the limit. The issue was only finally resolved when the future management pointed out that a 20:1 gearing limit would deny HMC any comparative advantage from its capital structure against that of its major competitors in the building society movement and would totally destroy the capital efficiency from which projected returns on this project were driven. This discussion clearly illustrated the significance placed on gearing by the investment community. By the time the equity raising process reached its conclusion, £31 million had been raised.

The first £20 million proved to be relatively straightforward, but the final £5 million more troublesome. Three potential investors were being canvassed to provide the final tranche and each was told that the first to reply positively would receive the entire allocation. One of the three said yes and the others were thanked for their interest but stood down. As is often the case with a financing proposal, once the requirement has been satisfied, those excluded become even more enthusiastic. Having spent nearly three months trying to reach a decision, both of the other two potential investors became so keen on the company within two days of being stood down that they demanded to be included. The company took the view that it would be foolish to turn down any offer of equity and consequently the books were closed at £31 million.

Equity structure

The initial equity was raised as a mixture of ordinary and preference share capital:

Ordinary shares	(557 500 @ 10p)	£55 750
Preference shares	(3 110 000 @ £10)	31 100 000
		£31 155 750

The ordinary shares were owned by the four main sponsors of the company together with two external non-executive directors, one of whom was Chairman. In addition, management was awarded options over a maximum of 1 million ordinary shares, which would represent between 8% and 12% of the company, the precise level of ownership depending on the financial performance of HMC.

The preference share capital was subscribed by 15 institutions split into three broad groups, namely, sponsors, strategic investors (institutions with an involvement or potential involvement in UK retail financial services) and venture capitalists. The preference shares carried an initial coupon of 5%, payable for the year to March 1988, the first full year of HMC's operations, rising annually by 1% until reaching 9% for the year to March 1992. The preference shares were then subject to mandatory conversion to ordinary shares upon the signing of HMC's March 1992 accounts. Both classes of share capital were subject to pre-emption rights in favour of existing shareholders.

The share capital was issued as fully paid in spite of HMC requiring only a small portion of the whole to commence business. It was felt that this was preferable to a partly paid structure, where banks providing warehouse finance might need to form a view of the shareholders' ability to meet future calls. This 'surplus capital' generated by the fully paid feature was one factor in the process, which eventually led to an ordinary/preference structure.

Surplus capital could be reinvested to provide preference shareholders with a running yield on their investment together with a degree of protection against dilution by the sponsors' ordinary shareholding. Nobody had a problem with dilution caused by the potential issuing of new shares as part of the incentive programme for managers but this was not true for any of the improved performance flowing to the sponsors. Hence, a high dividend strip before the ordinaries could participate, justified from the projections prepared by anticipated financial trading (MBS) profits.

Preference share problems

The early financial performance of the company was, as is often the case with start-up businesses, below initial expectations and the consequences for the preference dividend, the rights of the preference shareholders and the company were far reaching. The original financial projections had included an MBS trading profit stream, but although MBS trading had been envisaged as a core business, it was abandoned as a result of the high capital commitment necessary to run a trading portfolio and the lack of liquidity in the early days of the sterling MBS market. Far from being a financial trader which originated mortgages to provide its product, HMC became a mainstream mortgage lender.

Although the company was very successful in its new role, HMC had inherited an equity structure designed for a business that could provide instant profits and not one for which profits would flow only when a critical mass had been established over the longer term. Preference share structures are still used in similar circumstances but at HMC the preference shareholders owned such a large proportion of the company (up to 88% and many of them were also ordinary shareholders) that any argument for treating these shareholders differently from the rest was difficult to see. Furthermore, the level of coupon proved inordinately high for a new business, whose spectacular growth required more capital than expected, and the rising nature of the coupon meant that once HMC was behind in its payments, it had little chance of catching up.

HMC opened its doors for business in September 1986, and enjoyed a period of dramatic growth on the back of a very strong mortgage market as shown below.

Year	1987	1988	1989	1990	1991	1992
Total mortgage assets (£000s)	129 126	704 851	1 228 778	1 441 184	1 711 534	1 899 988
Pre-tax profits (£000s)	(2 505)	1 704	2 004	888	2 211	5 157

The absence of MBS trading profits meant that the preference dividend fell into arrears. This had little impact on the company's day-to-day business but produced an interesting problem after the mandatory conversion of the preference shares into ordinary shares. HMC's articles provided that any dividend arrears survived mandatory conversion, with the effect that arrears of £8.8 million continued to represent a prior charge on any profits of the company. The priorities in respect of capital were unclear and, as will be seen later, this point achieved a degree of prominence towards the end of HMC's independent existence.

Financing the business

Having raised £31 million of equity, HMC went about generating sufficient warehousing facilities to enable it to function on a day-to-day basis. Warehouse funding was always regarded as a facilitator of HMC's business, enabling the company to build up sufficient volumes of assets (£150 million) prior to refinancing in the MBS market.

The banking market was not thought of as an appropriate medium for financing mortgage loans with a contractual maturity of 25 years. Banks were able to provide three-, or sometimes five-, year facilities which granted HMC both the time to build volumes for re-financing and also the flexibility to choose the most opportune time to access the capital markets.

Warehouse financing lines remained constant at around £500 million throughout the life of the company as the balance sheet grew from £250 million to almost £2 billion. The keys to the financing strategy of the company were the ability to grow the balance sheet without growing the banking facilities and the avoidance of any significant refinancing risk by accessing the MBS market at every opportunity, something that many of HMC's competitors ignored to their cost. The capital commitment to warehouse finance was relatively high. Virtually every banking agreement, whether syndicated or bilateral, imposed a 20:1 gearing ratio with a further capital requirement for loans six months or more in arrears and a minimum capital requirement in the warehousing company of £1 million.

Capital strains

The combination of providing capital into the warehouse companies and into MBS issues, which had originally been thought to be capital free, together with the reduced level of profitability of the company meant that the initial £31 million of equity capital would soon be fully deployed. Management was reluctant to return to the shareholders for more equity for reasons of dilution and consequently explored other avenues to generate long-term capital.

HMC was eventually able to identify a single life company investor willing to purchase £20 million of long-term (20-year) loan stock. This stock was issued by the parent holding company at a coupon of 12.25% (3% over the then yield of the reference gilt), with the only substantial covenants being a parent company alone gearing restriction of 1.5 times net worth and a minimum net worth covenant of £25 million. The capital raised was able to be down-streamed to the warehouse and MBS issuing companies without any further restrictions, giving HMC, in effect, over £50 million of capital resources. This enabled the company to reach the stage where it became self-sufficient, i.e. future capital requirements were able to be satisfied out of retained profits.

Securitisation

HMC was only able to grow rapidly from nothing into a £2 billion business because of its use of the MBS markets. The financing strategy or the company was very simple – mortgage loans were warehoused in the banking markets and refinanced as soon as possible into the MBS market – and this strategy remained unchanged through every phase of HMC's development.

Some of HMC's competitors appeared to try to arbitrage the banking and MBS costs. But they failed to appreciate that bank and securitised debt are fundamentally different in nature and choosing between them on the grounds of price alone is rather like looking for a means of transport and buying a bike rather than a car because a bike is cheaper. The problem with this choice is that you get wet on a bike when it rains.

Securitised debt offered HMC four key advantages over conventional funding:

(i) Maturity finance
HMC's mortgage loans had nominal maturities typically in the 20–25 year range, but with early redemption completely at the discretion of the borrower. The company's liability structure needed to mirror the maturity profile of its assets and issuing MBS which returned principal to bondholders only to the extent that redemptions in the underlying securitised mortgage portfolio achieved a perfect match.

Refinancing risk in the business was limited to that portion of the assets which was funded out of the banking warehouse, generally around 10% of the total. This comfort was especially important for HMC which, as it was not a deposit-taking institution, operated outside of any protection afforded by a lender of last resort and it enabled HMC to manage a long period of disappearing liquidity in the banking markets from 1990 without any adverse effect on its new lending activities.

(ii) Diversification
Aside from the maturity considerations outlined above, it was crucial for the company not to have its lending constrained by running up against borrower or sector limits imposed by the banking markets.

There were times when it felt as if almost the entire banking market had decided to pull back from what became described as 'Anglo Saxon property lending' – a term embracing everything from speculative property development in Houston to lending to the major building societies in the UK. During this period, HMC never encountered any difficulties in having its MBS issues underwritten by the leading investment banks in the MBS market, nor in selling its securities to end investors. The vast bulk of HMC's MBS issuance was AAA rated with the result that the market always remained open and that access to that market became simply a question of price.

(iii) Efficient capital utilisation
Although the MBS market was not generally able to deliver premium pricing and hence 'capital free' funding, access to the market was nevertheless very capital efficient.

Capital free securitisation is a feature of the US MBS market, but one significant difference between the UK and US MBS markets is that the latter tends to be a fixed rate market, where premium pricing is not regarded as unusual, whilst the former is predominantly floating rate note (FRN) based. When HMC suggested to one distinguished British merchant banker that an FRN issue might carry a higher than market coupon with an above par issue price, he replied that he thought the market would regard this as 'rather vulgar, something that Southern European sovereign issuers sometimes resort to'.

A securitised issue uses very little capital (and here capital is defined in the broadest sense to include all cash outflows for fees and expenses, in addition to the capitalisation of the issuing vehicle) compared to finance provided by the banking markets. This meant that HMC's limited capital resources could be made to work extremely hard.

Given a standard banking gearing ratio of 20:1 and HMC's gearable capital of £50 million, a business funded exclusively by bank debt would have peaked at £1 billion of assets. By securitising virtually all of the company's assets, HMC was able to build a sustainable £2 billion business and still have unutilised capital resources available to support further growth.

A typical MBS transaction would involve the issue of £155 million securities and would cost something in the order of £1.25–1.5 million, producing a gearing ratio of between 100 and 120 times. The efficient utilisation of limited capital through securitisation was therefore the foundation on which HMC's business was based.

(iv) Enhanced returns on capital

The final compelling argument for securitisation concerned competitiveness and rates of return in the mortgage market.

HMC evaluated its MBS transactions using a number of criteria, the most significant of which was the rate of return on capital employed. It might be unusual to evaluate a financing transaction in terms of returns rather than costs, but HMC built and operated a complex cash flow model to predict the performance of a mortgage portfolio. A number of variables including expected redemption rates, arrears, mortgage margins and funding rates were used to model cash flows arising on a given portfolio financed with a particular MBS structure.

The initial capital requirement for a structure could then be compared with projected cash flows and expected returns calculated over a range of different assumptions. Generally, transactions giving rise to relatively high but stable returns on capital under a variety of different scenarios were effected.

Figure 4.4 compares the returns on capital available from a conventionally funded and securitised mortgage portfolio over a range of mortgage margins. The results of the capital efficiency of the

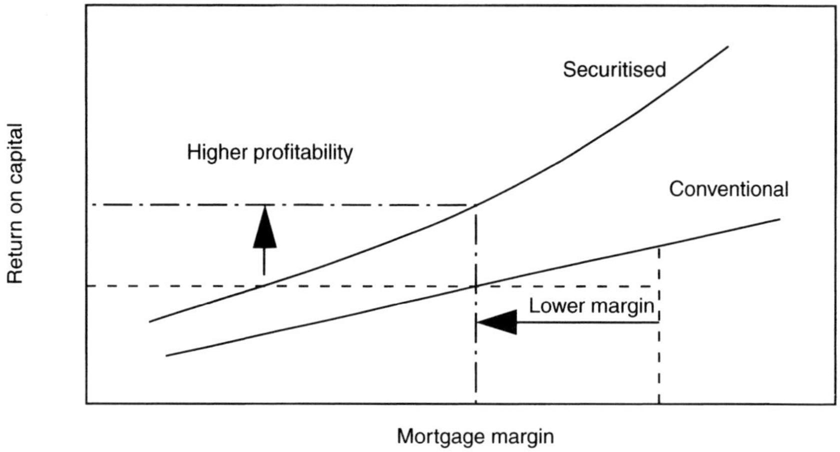

4.4 Return on capital.

securitisation process can be seen clearly from the chart. By securitising its assets, a lender can compete at lower margins and still generate greater profitability than a competitor which funds its assets in a conventional manner.

For HMC, securitisation represented far more than a prudent liability structure. The capital efficiency and profitability generated from securitising virtually the whole of the company's mortgage portfolio was consistent with HMC's corporate objectives of offering competitively priced mortgage products and achieving above average returns for shareholders.

The happy ending

An initial exit route for shareholders was intended to be available in the early 1990s via a market listing of HMC equity. The effects of the recession put paid to that plan, but HMC was able to prosper through this period for three main reasons:

(i) the strong credit culture, which permeated the company, meant that HMC was not hit as badly as some by repossessions and falling house prices;
(ii) the extensive use of securitisation enabled the company to navigate stormy times in the banking market and provided HMC with an extremely robust balance sheet structure; and

(iii) from June 1990, the company grew by acquisition as organic growth dried up.

HMC had been one of the first lenders to appreciate the benefits of portfolio acquisitions and had bid aggressively whenever portfolios came onto the market. By early 1994, portfolio prices had moved up considerably as other lenders sought to maintain their asset bases and in the light of this, HMC's management suggested that shareholders might like to explore a trade sale of the company to realise value as an alternative to listing.

Over 30 institutions expressed an interest in acquiring HMC and at the end of an exhaustive process an offer of over £70 million from Abbey National plc was recommended by the Board and accepted by the shareholders.

During this process, the question of the dividend arrears again came into the spotlight. All classes of shareholders accepted the former preference shareholders' rights to priority in any future dividend payments by the company, but the articles offered no guidance on how such rights should be treated in respect of an offer for the shares in the company. Former preference shareholders naturally took the view that their arrears should be cleared as a first call on the sale proceeds with the balance being distributed rateably amongst all shareholders. Others argued that the whole of the proceeds should simply be divided equally.

The potential transfer of value between old ordinary and old preference shareholders amounted to approximately £1 million, since former preference shareholders accounted for some 88% of the enlarged ordinary share capital. However this sum had a significant effect on the amount that would be received by former ordinary shareholders as it would increase or reduce their 12% share of proceeds by a considerable amount.

The issue was resolved by having Barings, HMC's financial advisers, value the preference entitlement by present valuing expected future dividend flows. This methodology attributed a value of approximately £4 million to the £8.8 million arrears and it was agreed that this element of the purchase consideration should be divided amongst former preference shareholders in proportion to their pre-conversion shareholdings.

HMC now operates as a separately branded subsidiary of Abbey National. Most of its former financing structures have been collapsed, since Abbey National does not operate under the severe capital rationing regimes of HMC, nor is maturity funding quite such an issue for a long established, large retail bank.

HMC's former shareholders were able to enjoy an acceptable return on their investments, especially in the light of the harsh business climate in which the company latterly had to operate. HMC's management had the satisfaction of seeing a business, which was built from nothing in 1986, prosper through difficult times and finally find a secure long-term role within a first class retail financial institution.

Chapter

5 The international dimension

Introduction

What happens when a corporation operates in more than one country? This chapter looks at the balance sheet implications for such companies and examines related financial issues such as taxation and funding. It explains why international companies often have complex financial structures and sets out some of the advantages and disadvantages of such structures.

Note: This chapter was written before the UK Budget 2000 and went to press before the draft Finance Bill has been published. At this stage it is clear that the role of dividend mixer companies (see below) is under review by the UK authorities. However, or the purposes of this volume no allowance for the impact of the outline changes has been made.

Background

Corporations usually enter international markets in search of profit. If they wish to trade in a new country, they must learn the trading customs of that market as they will often have a new currency to manage, and they will have to cope with a host of reporting, regulatory, tax and social issues. They will then have to choose the most appropriate and practical solutions for acquiring, financing and managing the business.

The average chief financial officer is likely to have specific requirements relating to domestic financing, which boil down to the minimising of after-tax costs, always provided that this does not involve unacceptable covenants. When dealing with overseas affiliates, the financial management of a group will focus on: holding structure, tax and funding; control issues; and accounting.

Holding structure, tax and funding

The group must ensure that finance is available to meet commercial needs and that the appropriate corporate structures are established for tax purposes, bearing in mind the need to avoid associated managerial constraints. The intention is that tax and financial charges payable by the group should be kept to the minimum level reasonably possible.

Control issues

The directors of the group need to be sure that its financial affairs are well managed. In particular, guidelines for the identification and control of tax and treasury-related risks should be established and monitored. Such risks and controls would include:

- ensuring that staff are well trained good reporting systems, which are separate from dealing functions, are established, proper controls are in place and clear audit trails are established;
- preventing loss due to market movements or regulatory changes;
- preventing inefficiency or fraud;
- ensuring before an investment is made in a new jurisdiction that cash can be repatriated when needed by way of dividends or otherwise without loss of value.

This requires good planning, forecasting and reporting, and in particular, the review of all projects by the tax, accounting, legal and treasury functions at an early stage.

Accounting

The group must produce reported consolidated profits, which satisfy shareholders and equity analysts on the one hand and lenders, banks and credit-rating agencies on the other. There should be no surprises arising from unforeseen changes in profitability due to the movement of foreign exchange rates, interest rates or tax rates.

Holding structure

When reporting its results, a multinational corporation will often present a simple picture of two or three different businesses whose overall performance and profitability are analysed in detail. Would that the legal structures and funding issues were so simple in practice.

While making a presentation at a conference, the treasurer of a multinational chemical corporation briefly showed a blueprint of its international corporate structure of equity and debt. This blueprint was considerably more complex than the average wiring diagram – a tangled web of companies, shareholdings, inter-company loans and external financing across the globe. It appears to be the case that managing successfully the finances of an overseas operation requires, first, the analysis of complex funding, currency and tax matters, and, secondly, the ability to put the right debt and equity structures and frameworks in place to deliver tangible benefits.

When a company plans to create branches or acquire overseas subsidiaries or assets, the structure will be affected by the profitability of these overseas operations, both current and projected. This creates opportunities for tax planning. If the legal system of the country in question is highly litigious in character, then it will be more common to split the operation into a large number of small companies to protect the larger group from legal attack. It may also be considered desirable to set up legal structures that would enable the parent easily to dispose of subsidiary groups for strategic reasons. Corporate structures will therefore be determined by business requirements, by tax and by legal requirements.

Costs

Financial costs associated with overseas operations can be summarised into two categories: those that should be identified at an early stage and managed; and those that are unexpected and have to be dealt with. The more costs that arise in the former category the better. Changes in tax legislation in the UK, Holland or the US have left many a clever tax plan high and dry, with cash located in the wrong jurisdiction and no chance of repatriating it unless a punitive tax charge is incurred. The movement of cash between jurisdictions needs to be managed carefully to ensure that the tax costs are minimised. Expensive withholding taxes may often be minimised by the use of appropriate tax treaty provisions. Dividends paid between companies resident in European Union (EU) countries can now generally be paid without withholding taxes following the implementation of the EU Parent/Subsidiary Directive. Careful planning can, therefore, pay handsome dividends.

Managers of international groups can reduce financial costs to a large extent by taking advantage of central purchasing power. By negotiating through a group treasury or a central finance function, bank charges, foreign exchange dealing costs, audit fees and borrowing or investment margins can all be minimised. For it may be from funding may be from local sources such as bank finance or leasing, inter-company loan or equity investment. Generally speaking, however, it is cheaper for a group to borrow centrally through its treasury and provide the funds to a subsidiary by way of inter-company debt or equity than it is for the subsidiary to borrow in the open market. Local borrowings would be more common for joint ventures or in countries with exchange controls or a high political risk.

Central co-ordination of a group's overseas activities throughout the world can give rise to several commercial advantages, such as the management of exchange exposures, and can also give opportunities for some sensible tax management.

Holding companies located in jurisdictions such as the Netherlands, Luxemburg or Switzerland can be used for such central co-ordination and to avoid tax on capital gains realised by selling subsidiaries, while also assisting the effective use of foreign tax credits. Delaware holding companies in the US can ensure that corporate operations connected with the raising of debt on the US financial markets can be structured to minimise state tax liabilities. However, in most cases there is the need to ensure that the overseas holding company is managed and controlled locally, which has consequential costs.

Tax

After the commercial decision to investigate an overseas venture has been taken, there are a number of questions which need to be asked about the true state of the overseas company's business and the regulatory framework of the country concerned. The tax system in the jurisdiction will be one of the most important areas for consideration.

In general, the aim of a finance director is to ensure that the group does not pay taxes world-wide that exceed the domestic tax rate (currently 30%). This will be achieved principally by obtaining the maximum credit for foreign taxes actually paid and receiving the maximum deduction for losses incurred. More ambitious structures will seek to earn and retain profit in low-taxed overseas jurisdictions, although anti-avoidance legislation may make this difficult to achieve. Corporations could reasonably expect that tax deductions would be available in respect of capital expenditure and operating losses and that this would reduce the corporation's tax charge. This is not always the case. Deductions for interest expense, for example, are not always available. It is also the case that tax mitigation in one country can sometimes cause adverse effects in another country, so it is important not only to deal with experts within each jurisdiction, but with individuals who have experience internationally. The finance director will need to be reassured that tax arrangements are sound at the point they are established and will need continual confirmation that tax structures are still robust as time goes by. It should also be borne in mind that the robustness of a structure will normally be assessed in a tax audit on a retrospective rather than a current basis and will be judged by the attitudes applying at the time of audit rather than those at the time of creation. Caution should therefore be exercised.

Tax residence

Governments always need money. In a perfect world, a company that makes profits will expect to have a fair proportion of those profits subjected to income taxes at a reasonable rate. Governments are aware that corporations will attempt to minimise taxes paid and therefore weight the rules in their own favour. The rule in the UK, for example, is that a company that is tax resident in the UK is liable to corporation tax on its world-wide income and profits, wherever arising. Tax residence in the UK is determined by incorporation or location of central management and control. Thus, a company incorporated in the UK will be treated as resident for tax purposes. A company that is not incorporated in the UK but is centrally managed in the UK will also be treated as being resident for tax purposes. However, other countries may also attempt to tax the same profits either because their rules of company residence are different from those of the UK or because the UK company operates in a third country through a branch or agency. The prospect of economic double taxation then rears its head, and this exposure needs to be managed.

Double tax relief

It is generally recognised (unitary tax in the state of California and some other US states being noticeable exceptions) that corporations should not be taxed twice on the same income. Therefore, under UK law, in general a corporation will be entitled to a credit for overseas tax paid against UK tax chargeable on the same profits. This credit, known as double tax relief, is limited, however, to the lower of the overseas tax rate or the UK rate on the same profits. Where the overseas rate is greater than the UK rate, there is no direct method of obtaining a refund on the excess tax, though there is a potential solution if there is an intermediate holding company in the structure as described below.

Double tax treaties

Like the UK, the majority of countries have a form of double tax relief enshrined in domestic legislation, but there is a network of some 2000 international treaties that also offer double tax relief. The majority of the tax treaties are based on an OECD model, which was developed in 1977, though every treaty is different.

The treaties are designed to prevent double taxation, to prevent the evasion of taxes by exchange of information between the two countries and to regulate the taxation treatment of various sources of income such as business profits, dividends, royalties, rental and interest payments. The interest, dividend and royalty provisions of double tax treaties are most commonly referred to in order to determine the extent to which withholding taxes on cash flows between the two jurisdictions are to be mitigated. The other important article is the business profits or permanent establishment article, which is used to define whether an activity within a country is regarded as a 'permanent establishment' and hence taxable in that country. The term usually incorporates a place of management such as an office, workshop or factory, but a company can be deemed to have a permanent establishment if an agent or employee has the authority to conclude contracts in the name of the overseas enterprise.

Comprehensive tax treaties tend to be those agreed between developed countries with high tax rates. Agreements with countries operating as tax havens tend to be more limited in nature. Hence, with careful consideration of double tax relief provisions, whether unilateral or bilateral, many of the problems associated with double taxation can be avoided.

Structuring foreign activities

Branch

When starting a new venture overseas, the operation is frequently established as a branch. This has a number of advantages:

- it is relatively simple and may well have lower running costs by avoiding statutory requirements such as audits;
- it usually avoids the need to pay capital duty;
- initial losses can frequently be absorbed by the parent in the home country and, in some countries (such as the UK), these losses can be carried forward indefinitely;
- repatriation of profits can frequently be made to the parent company without suffering withholding tax.

The operations can be incorporated (i.e. set up as a subsidiary company) at a later stage when it starts to be profitable, though there is sometimes an exit tax charge associated with this.

When acquiring an existing operation, the purchaser will decide whether they wish to acquire assets or to acquire the company as a going concern. Acquiring assets is cleaner from a legal perspective and can allow for improved tax depreciation if it is possible to revalue the assets for tax purposes (although some jurisdictions do pass certain legal liabilities together with the assets). It will often be more expensive to achieve than the acquisition of a company, however, either because of higher transfer taxes or because the vendor will suffer a higher tax charge on sale and will expect to be compensated for this. There are a number of benefits to operating a subsidiary company in the chosen jurisdiction.

- Local businesses and customers may prefer dealing with a company resident in that country rather than a branch of an overseas company. This applies in the US capital markets, where US investors tend to favour domestic issuers.
- Usually profits made in that country will be taxed in the parent country only when transferred back as a dividend. At worst, there will be a timing advantage, at best the tax may not be payable at all.
- If the country has a high tax rate, the company can be financed with inter-company loans provided that the interest is allowed to be tax deductible.

Intermediate companies

It can be seen from the above that the taxable profits of the foreign operation (and the profits of its affiliates), both actual and projected, are of key importance when considering the holding and financing structure. There may be a number of commercial and tax advantages in holding the overseas investment in a subsidiary company through an intermediate holding or finance company. Historically, many UK companies have used a Dutch sub-holding company to hold their investments overseas. The Netherlands has an excellent infrastructure for managing the activities of international groups as well as an excellent tax treaty network, and there is substantial shareholding in an active company, a friendly regime in the form of the 'participation exemption', which does not tax capital gains realised by selling subsidiaries. More recently, because of unfavourable changes in the US/Dutch treaty and increasingly unfriendly attitudes within the Dutch authorities, alternative jurisdictions with similar regimes such as Luxemburg and Switzerland have started to come into favour. Intermediate holding companies are sometimes called dividend mixer companies because the effect under UK tax law of receiving a number of dividends indirectly through one company is that dividends from high and low taxing jurisdictions can be combined (although there was a proposal – strongly resisted – in the UK 2000 Finance Bill that this should change).

Dividend mixing – an example

A UK company has a marginal tax rate of 30%. It has domestic profits of 1000 and receives equal dividends from two subsidiaries, one from a country where the domestic tax rate is 55% and the other where the domestic tax rate is 25%. On the dividend from income taxed at 55%, the parent will receive a 30% tax credit and not pay any further tax. On the dividend from income taxed at 25%, the parent will receive a 25% credit but be taxed a further 5% in the UK so that the overall tax rate is 30% on the dividend

Table 5.1 Tax paid without dividend mixing

	£
Domestic income	1000
Income from country A (55% tax rate)	1000
Income from country B (25% tax rate)	1000
	3000
Tax at 30%	900
Double tax relief 30% of 1000	300
25% of 1000	250
UK tax payable	350
Note: overseas tax paid	800
Total tax paid	1150 (38.3%)

Table 5.2 Tax paid using dividend mixer

	£
Domestic income	1000
Income from Dutch mixer	2000
	3000
Tax at 30%	900
Double tax relief 30% of 2000	600
UK tax payable	300
Note overseas tax paid	800
Total tax paid	1100 (36.7%)

from the low-tax jurisdiction. The overall rate of tax paid is 30% on domestic income, 55% on the one dividend and 30% on the other – an average of roughly 38.3%. This is illustrated in Table 5.1.

If shares are held through an intermediate holding company, such as a Dutch company, and dividends are paid to it and then onward dividended to the parent, a better result arises. The UK parent receives a dividend from The Netherlands that has a 40% tax credit attached to it because, first, the dividends are not taxed in Holland. Secondly, tax has been paid at 55% on one half and 25% on the other giving an average rate of 40% overall, and so there is no further tax to pay on the income. This is shown in Table 5.2.

The result is that there is no further UK tax liability on the dividend with the underlying credit of 25%, and the overall tax rate for the group in cash and profit and loss account terms has been reduced by approximately 1.3%. Figure 5.1 shows the flows of dividends that take place.

The Netherlands is one country that is used for such a holding company. Austria, Luxemburg, Denmark and Switzerland can also be used, though their networks of international tax treaties are less extensive. Other companies may have finance subsidiaries in Ireland, Belgium or Puerto Rico because of the tax incentives offered there. Within mainland US, Delaware holding companies are established to avoid local state taxes, which are not subject to international treaties.

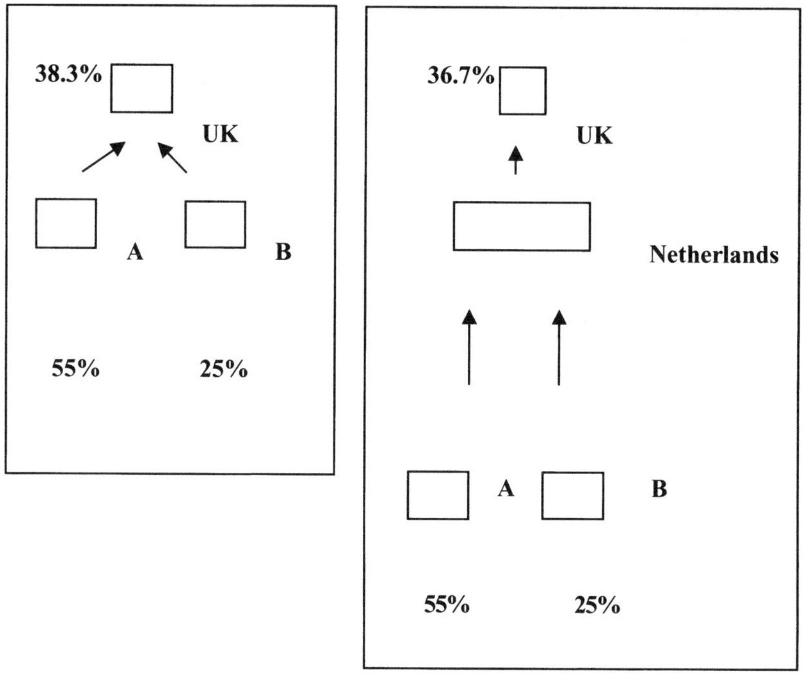

5.1 Dutch mixer company: dividend flows and marginal tax rate in each jurisdiction.

However, it should never be forgotten that the framework of international treaties is constantly changing, driven by the desire to conserve tax revenue and perceptions of abuse by treaty partners to obtain a competitive advantage. The 1993 US/Dutch tax treaty, for example, potentially exposed all dividends received by a Dutch holding company from its US subsidiary, to a 30% withholding tax on top of the 40% tax on profits already paid in the US. A number of non-US corporations have established Delaware finance operations to issue debt in the US because such US investors prefer to lend to domestic companies. The use of a Delaware company also ensures that local taxes will not be payable on the finance company's income. However, the introduction of the treaty mean that with the imposition of withholding taxes, loans from the US to The Netherlands may no longer be tax effective, unless some substantial 'presence' requirements in The Netherlands can be satisfied.

In the Fig. 5.2, a US holding company is shown. A further reason for an intermediate holding company would be to ensure that there is a consolidated group for tax purposes in a particular jurisdiction. Tax consolidation is available in many countries but it can take a long time to obtain, particularly if the common parent is outside the jurisdiction. Accordingly, it is often more sensible to have a single holding company within one country, which will hold shares in local operating subsidiaries, unless there are plans

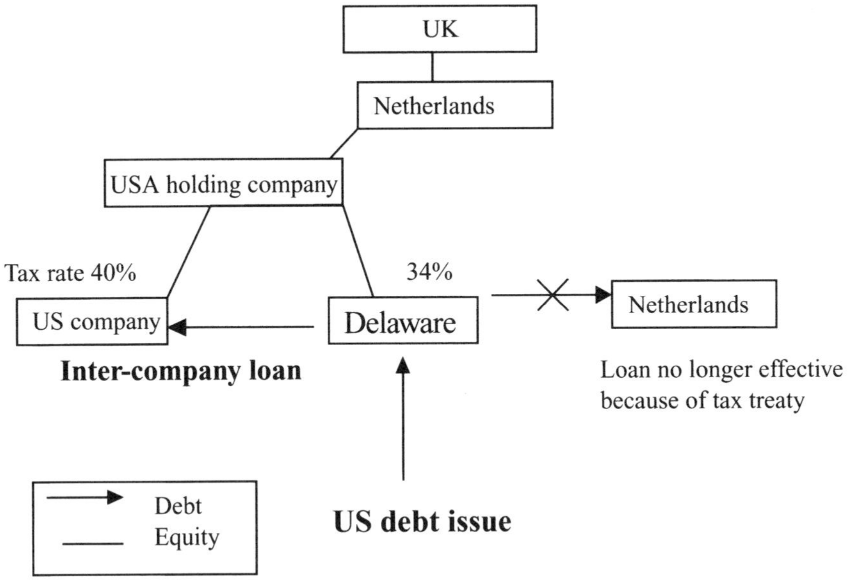

5.2 Using a US holding company.

to sell one of the companies included, when additional capital gains exposures can arise.

Adjusting profits

There are a number of techniques that a multinational organisation can adopt to repatriate overseas profits. These techniques can also be used to reduce taxable profits or use up tax losses in one jurisdiction or another. The following are common areas for consideration when looking to affect profits:

- payment for goods and services between related companies;
- charging a management fee for central support services;
- licensing of intellectual or other intangible rights, which may be used by an overseas subsidiary in exchange for royalty payments;
- paying a guarantee fee to the parent company for guaranteeing local debt facilities;
- financing by way of inter-company or external debt instead of equity (Fig. 5.3).

Taxing authorities are keen to ensure that corporations do not abuse these methods of managing profits, so they look in particular at four areas: transfer pricing; thin capitalisation; controlled foreign companies (CFC); and Treasury Consent.

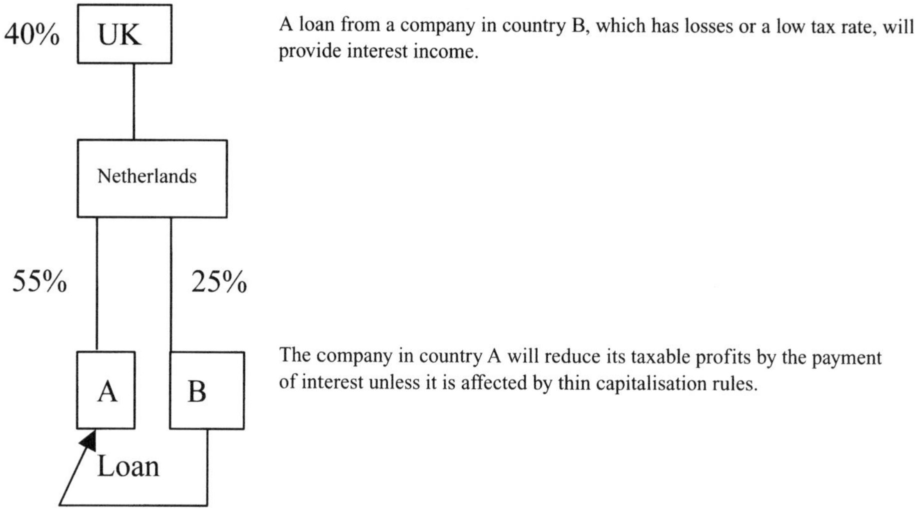

5.3 Inter-company funding example.

Transfer pricing

If the payments to or from an affiliate are considered out of line with an arms' length commercial rate, then an adjustment will be made. This adjustment could apply to the cost of goods, the percentage rate of a royalty or the rate of interest payable on a loan. In certain countries such as the UK and the US, it is essential therefore to keep detailed contemporaneous records to demonstrate that the payment is at an open market rate.

Thin capitalisation

If the proportion of debt to equity gets too high, many jurisdictions will deny the deduction of part or all of the interest expense against taxable profits. Companies with very high levels of debt are referred to as being thinly capitalised. For example, many countries have rules that deny deductions for interest expense on the excess of debt over a 3:1 debt/equity ratio. In the US, thin capitalisation rules known as 'earnings stripping regulations' were originally introduced in 1989, and have since been amended to meet the popular conception that Japanese companies were not paying sufficient tax on profits earned in the US.

The US rules are particularly tight. They treat debt lent to an American company by an overseas affiliate as 'tainted' and only permit corporations with a debt/equity ratio greater than 1.5:1 to deduct interest on inter-company loans if the interest is covered twice by operating profits before interest, amortisation and taxes. Of relevance is the fact that if the US company has external debt (such as money raised on the US domestic and international capital markets) guaranteed by the non-US parent company, that will also count as 'tainted' debt. This has reduced the appetite for domestic US capital market issues by non-US issuers in recent times. There is no UK definition of an acceptable debt/equity ratio, but it is believed that ratios in excess of two or three to one, would be likely to be challenged, depending on the level of interest cover.

Controlled foreign companies

Both the UK and the US have anti-avoidance legislation relating to overseas affiliates. The intention of the UK legislation is to require certain overseas holding companies or operating companies in low-tax jurisdictions (defined as one where the effective rate of tax is less than 75% of the UK rate) to pay tax on the proportion of profits attributable to UK corporate shareholders with at least a 25% interest in the CFC, calculated on the basis of UK taxation.

There are a number of exemptions from this requirement. One is an 'exempt activities' test. The exempt activities test basically exempts the majority of 'normal' trading companies from the legislation, provided that they are trading in goods and services with third parties, and also certain classes of holding company. Another is the 'acceptable distribution policy' test. Under this test, exemptions will be obtained if an affiliate distributes 90% of post-tax profits, calculated on the basis of UK tax principles, are remitted to the UK. This could have the effect of recouping tax depreciation granted to the subsidiary of a UK company based in a foreign jurisdiction. For example, a Dutch company must recalculate the profit ignoring the tax depreciation on the trademark, which is not deductible in the UK. The same legislation can catch interest-free loans between overseas affiliates, which may be permitted abroad, but are not considered to be at arm's length pricing for UK tax purposes. UK CFC legislation does not apply to capital gains unless they could be assessed as trading profits under UK tax law principles.

Generally speaking, a holding company that only receives dividends from exempt companies is not subject to the CFC rules. From the discussion above, it is clear that a group must ensure that tax deductions that are permitted overseas, but not in the UK, are taken in companies which are not subject to, or are exempt from, the UK CFC legislation.

Treasury consent

Taxing authorities like to keep a close watch on the movements of money around a group. In the UK, S765 of the Income and Corporate Tax Act (ICTA) 1988 requires companies to obtain approval in advance from the Inland Revenue (known as Treasury Consent) for certain inter-company loans or equity investments into group companies outside the EU. Within the EU, notification must be given within the subsequent six months. Failure to obtain such approval is a criminal offence, so this is a matter which will usually be taken seriously by the finance director!

In summary, the structure that a company will use to hold and finance an overseas operation will therefore depend on a number of tax issues:

- profitability in each country (current and expected);
- where resident for tax purposes – this depends on the country of incorporation or the location of central management and control;
- the tax regime in both countries (current and expected);
- tax treaties;
- whether trading or investment companies and the effect of CFC legislation;
- the pricing of the transfer of goods and services between jurisdictions.

The desire to provide a sensible framework to maximise after-tax profits is probably the biggest single reason for complicated corporate structures.

Control issues

Confidence is said to be the feeling you get just before you really understand the problem. Control should be the way in which the finance director can identify a potential problem and stop it happening in the first place.

This is not always easy. The finance director will need to check that the major financial risks relating to international operations have been considered. From an accounting perspective, there is the need to ensure an adequate financial and management reporting structure. From a treasury perspective, there are a number of potential danger areas, such as:

- inadequate reporting and control of cash;
- unexpected exposures – this can cover interest rate risk, foreign exchange risk, counter-party risk and political risks;
- ignorance of treasury risks – the danger that a transaction will be undertaken where the potential consequences were not clearly understood or reported at the start;
- unauthorised dealing;
- fraud, theft or negligence;
- inadequate procedures and controls.

From a practical viewpoint, it is not usually possible for a finance director in the parent country to police all these issues. A degree of control can be exercised by centralising all treasury operations as far as possible in one place, but it also has its limitations, particularly in a commercial organisation that operates in different time zones. The appropriate location of a central treasury can also have tax advantages. It is therefore essential that clear guidelines should be established, monitored by local management and regularly checked, if appropriate, by the internal audit department to ensure that cash is well managed and that potential risks are identified.

The guidelines may set out among other issues:

- a payment risk and compliance section with guidelines as to who is entitled to operate bank accounts and authorise the transfer of cash;
- the type of financial instruments that may be used (for example, no use of derivatives products except by central group treasury);
- guidelines for prudent cash and foreign exchange management worldwide. This includes bank relationships and criteria for acceptable counterparties. For example, it might be prudent to use banks with A credit ratings (or better) from the major credit rating agencies. This does, however, bring problems in areas where the local banks do not have credit ratings from a major credit rating agency, or have ratings that do not meet the counter-party criteria set by the Board;
- the need for all parts of the organisation to be aware of treasury-related risks and involve the treasury in new overseas projects at an early stage of planning, and the need to encourage training in treasury-related issues throughout the group;
- the need to encourage joint venture partners to adopt the same prudent approach even where the shareholding in the joint venture is less than 50%;
- the need to save costs by regularly reviewing financial expenses such as bank charges and centralising cash whenever practical.

It may also be useful to set out guidelines for acceptable covenants in loan documents. When an organisation operates within one country, it will negotiate loan terms and conditions. Subsidiaries overseas may not enjoy the same credit strength. External lenders will therefore attempt either to negotiate a guarantee or letter of support from the parent group or to negotiate loan covenants and borrowing margins that reflect the weaker credit strength of the borrower. From a control perspective, there are two concerns for the parent. Loan covenants may be drawn too tightly, triggering a default which may have a knock-on effect for the parent company, and the giving of a guarantee or letter of comfort may have other consequences, tax or legal. In Australia, for example, the courts may view a letter of comfort (even one which specificically states that it creates no legal obligations) as having the strength of a guarantee. One area of control that needs to be kept in mind are the tax arrangements established for the management of overseas holding companies. On the one hand, such companies should undertake transactions that are for the benefit of the group as a whole such as to purchase equity holdings, make dividends and inter-company loans, make payments of various kinds and generally to act in the best interests of its shareholders. On the other hand, many countries, including the UK, have tests that will tax overseas companies as domestic companies if they believe that control rests effectively in the UK. Care needs to be taken, therefore, in the establishment and management of holding companies overseas, and the right balance struck between local control and the needs of the group.

Perhaps some of the most difficult control problems are those caused by governmental organisations such as the EU. For example, protecting a corporation from foreign exchange variations in the price of agricultural products within the European Community is difficult because the pricing mechanism, though much simplified with the introduction of the Euro, still seems designed more to protect farmers' income than to provide a system that reflects open market currency movements. Dealing with a depreciating currency in Brazil is difficult, especially at times when the free movement of capital is blocked. Operating in China successfully today depends to a large extent on obtaining the trust of the local bank manager and leaving him to interpret central regulations in a helpful way. Comparative shopping for financial services in some countries is frowned on as a sign of bad faith in the financial community.

As a matter of practice, the best way to handle control issues is from a bottom-up rather than a top-down perspective. Those companies that involve management and staff on a continuous basis in the identification of financial risk, reporting, amendment of guidelines and subsequent training, will achieve far better results from a control and a performance perspective than those organisations that approve a sensible set of working guidelines, then breathe a sigh of relief, put the guidelines into a cupboard and only review them when the next well-publicised disaster takes place.

Accounts

The group will wish to produce profits from its international operations which meet investor or creditor expectations. Can it be assumed that the accounts of all overseas companies within the group do reflect a true and fair view of the company's activities (it is said that there are now computerised accounting packages available in some countries that draw up different sets of accounts for presentation to management, accountants and others)? One problem is that official financial accounting and reporting practices can vary significantly from country to country. The emphasis of the accounts and the regulations that determine those accounts are dependent on whether the country is driven by an equity culture or by a debt culture, in other words whether the main users of the accounts are stock-market driven or are creditor driven. In their paper 'Accounting and credit analysis', Sarah Martin and Chiara Saliba (CS First Boston, December 1994) set out a table which summarises these cultures (Table 5.3).

Table 5.3 Summary of accounting cultures

	Stock market-driven	**Creditor-driven**
Main user group	Outside shareholders	Trade and bank creditors, employees
User interest	'True and fair' earnings measures, performance control of management	'Conservative' asset and liability valuations, coverage of liabilities by assets.
Primary focus	Profit and loss account	Balance sheet
Key measures	EPS (UK)/ROE	Solidity and solvency
Influential bodies	Accounting body, stock exchange regulator	State
Disclosure	Frequent and detailed	Less frequent and less detailed
Flexibility	High	Low

Reproduced by kind permission of CS First Boston.

In the view of Martin and Saliba, the UK and The Netherlands approximate the shareholder-driven culture, while continental Europe tends to resemble the creditor-driven culture. The US shows characteristics from both archetypes of accounting culture. The Japanese also represent a hybrid between these cultures.

Differences between jurisdictions abound:

- intangible assets may be permitted as a balance sheet asset and may be allowable for tax purposes;
- the definition of obligations which should be included on a balance sheet varies from country to country;
- fixed assets should not be revalued in certain jurisdictions, notably the US, where they are shown at historic cost. In other jurisdictions, upward revaluations are permitted and, in the UK, investment properties must be carried at open market values;
- the accounting for foreign exchange rates varies considerably. Some countries permit the matching of foreign exchange assets and liabilities, others require revaluation of the liability but not the asset. Some require unrealised foreign exchange gains and losses to be reflected through the profit and loss account while others allow profits or losses to be deferred until realised. The rate at which companies will translate foreign currency amounts (closing, average, historic or forward rate) will also vary.

Perhaps the most extreme example of a deferred foreign exchange loss was the $1 billion lost in 1993 by Showa Shell of Japan. The company undertook dollar/yen contracts in the late 1980s and continued to value them in the accounts at the original rates (as permitted under Japanese accounting practice) while the yen strengthened dramatically in the market-place. Closing the contracts cost the group dearly.

It is therefore important that all parts of an organisation realise that actions taken in an overseas jurisdiction may have unexpected implications for the consolidated accounts of the parent group. The finance director may well be charged with ensuring that local financial management are aware of the accounting rules in the parent company's country. The last thing that a finance director wants to see is some clever, off-balance sheet financing, which has to be put back on balance sheet unexpectedly so that forecasts given to, say, the credit-rating agencies, are not met. Nor does an equity analyst in a shareholder-driven culture, such as the UK, want to see large, unexpected losses due to currency fluctuations (though why this should be a problem, given that movement in currencies are so widely reported, is something of a mystery). The effect of foreign currency movements on the accounts, therefore, needs to be considered further.

Translation effects on consolidated accounts

Foreign currency is a key concern in the management of overseas operations and the reporting of the accounts. In some cases, it will be an important factor in the decision to invest in overseas subsidiaries. Japanese manufacturers, for example, have moved their production from Japan to other jurisdictions because the strength of the yen has increased production costs in relative terms beyond the point where production in Japan can be competitive. In other cases, foreign currency will not be important in the original investment decision when compared with the commercial considerations, but subsequent currency movements will have considerable effect on the profitability of the overseas operation when translated into the parent organisation's base currency. The effect on the accounts of a movement in exchange rates between one reporting date and the next is known as translation exposure.

This should be contrasted with the more familiar kind of foreign exchange exposure, known as transaction exposure. This arises where there is a time gap between the creation of an obligation to pay or receive a foreign currency and the delivery of the cash. The exposure exists because exchange rates will vary during the intervening period in a relatively unpredictable way. The difference between transaction exposure and translation exposure is that the former is directly concerned with the payment or receipt of cash, while translation exposure is not directly concerned with cash but only with the valuation of profits, assets and liabilities as reported in the accounts. Translation exposures will only become cash exposures in an indirect manner, for example, when a foreign currency asset or liability is disposed of. It may also happen when tax is charged on unrealised foreign currency gains and losses, or possibly (this is certainly a concern to some organisations) when an unexpected foreign exchange loss is reported, which causes a crisis of confidence among investors, and the share price of the group is adversely affected.

To illustrate how such translation exposures arise, take the example of a company operating in France. GooseCo SA is a small company involved in the production of golden eggs. Its balance sheet is a simple one, we show it both in Euros and translated into sterling at Euro (€) 1 = £0.60.

GooseCo	Assets	Liabilities		Assets	Liabilities	
	€000s			£000s		
	100	34	Debt	60	20	Debt
		66	Equity		40	Equity
	100	100		60	60	

The company is profitable, with operating income of €28 000 less interest of €1000 (3% on a loan of €34 000) producing net income of some €27 000 per annum. It attracts the attention of a UK egg producer, Gander PLC, which is a small public company quoted on the London Stock Exchange. Gander PLC's balance sheet is as follows.

Gander PLC	Assets	Liabilities	
	£000s		
	300	75	Debt
		225	Equity
	300	300	

Gander's operations and sales are currently entirely UK based, so all assets and liabilities are in sterling. An offer of €133 000 (£80 000) is made and accepted by the owners of GooseCo, and the French company becomes a subsidiary of the UK corporation.

In planning the acquisition, the finance director of Gander had decided that it was appropriate to borrow Euros, rather than issuing equity or borrowing sterling and then buying Euros. A loan facility of €167 000 (£100 000) would enable Gander to pay for the initial purchase, with sufficient in addition to be lent to GooseCo as an inter-company loan to replace GooseCo's €34 000 (£24 000) loan from its French bank.

As a result, the group balance sheet would be as follows.

Gander PLC	Assets	Liabilities	
	£000s		
Sterling assets	300	75	Sterling debt
Euro assets	60	100	Euro debt
		185	Equity
	360	360	

NB. The acquisition creates goodwill of £40 000. In the balance sheet shown above, this has been written off against reserves, being common historic practice in the UK and permitted in The Netherlands and Germany. In other countries (and now in the UK), such goodwill would appear on the balance sheet as an asset and be written off over its useful life through the profit and loss account. The period of such write-off does not normally exceed 20 years, though 40 years is currently the permitted maximum in the US (although this is under review). If goodwill remains on the balance sheet it will appear as follows:

Gander PLC	Assets	Liabilities	
	£000s		
Sterling assets	300	75	Sterling debt
Euro assets	60	100	Euro debt
Goodwill	40	225	Equity
	400	400	

The profit and loss account for the group will be (000s):

Gander PLC			£000s
Operating profit	Sterling		20
	Euro	€28 000	17
Earnings before interest and tax (EBIT)			37
Interest on £75 000	Sterling @ 6%		(4)
Interest on €167 000	€ @ 3%		(3)
Net PBT			30

The above profits are based on a €1 = £0.60 exchange rate. However, the finance director of Gander PLC needs to consider the effect of foreign exchange movements on its reported profits and balance sheet equity. Key concerns are:

- the sterling value of Euro profits will vary in an unpredictable manner as the exchange rate moves;
- covenants given to lenders in the group's loan documentation may be breached;
- results from trading operations as shown in the local currency financial statements may be distorted by gains and losses on the reported valuation of foreign currency assets and liabilities, which have to be charged through the profit and loss account.

Taking each of these in turn:

The sterling value of Euro profits will vary in an unpredictable manner
When GooseCo's financial accounts were produced only in Euros, foreign currency movements were not relevant to the profitability of the company. GooseCo is a Euro business with assets, liabilities, income and expenditure in that currency. However, once this company is owned by a foreign company, the movement of the Euro against the parent company's accounting currency will be an important factor to consider. The net Euro profits or losses will be translated into the parent's currency at the financial year-end rate or at an average rate for the financial year, according to accounting convention.

Since foreign exchange rates can regularly fluctuate by 20% in any one year, and movements of 40% are by no means uncommon, the reported profits of the subsidiary translated into the currency of the parent company could vary considerably from year to year. In a shareholder culture such as the UK, company boards are pleased to see profits flattered by windfall foreign exchange gains, but will be reluctant to see profits significantly reduced by foreign exchange movements. GooseCo's €28 000 profits are about £22 000 when reported at €1 = £0.80, but about £11 000 at €1 = £0.40.

To the man in the street, it seems entirely reasonable that a French goose company, selling its eggs in central France, should be funded in Euros. When a domestic company is taken over by a foreign parent, however, the currency of the funding is often changed and a translation currency exposure consequently arises. The obvious way to avoid such an exposure is to continue to fund in the local currency (in this case Euros) and also to fund the additional goodwill in the local currency. This movement in the foreign currency profits translated into sterling will be partly or completely mitigated by the movement in foreign currency interest when translated into sterling.

Funding in local currency may be the best way of reducing the risk that reported profits will fluctuate, but some companies prefer to manage their exposure to movements in reported foreign currency profits by the use of financial instruments. For example, a UK company in the services industry with considerable Euro income has been known to hedge its reported sterling profits by buying currency options. The company took the view that since the cost of the options was known in advance, the minimum sterling value of the reported Euro profits could be ascertained with certainty and that, therefore, the profit expectations of the financial community would be met. The company was therefore paying out cash to improve its book profits, which was seen to be a vital consideration in maintaining investor confidence. The observer might remark that it is a curious approach to cover a reported (non-cash) exposure with a cash payment. It is clearly better for management to hedge reported foreign currency profits with interest on foreign currency debt. It is also wise to manage investor expectations so that a movement in reported profits due to currency fluctuations does not impact confidence.

To illustrate the position, consider the reported profits of Gander PLC, which in the current year are £28 000, with Euro income translated at €1 = £0.60. If the company changes its debt so that all £175 000 borrowings are denominated in sterling, then its reported profits will vary substantially as the exchange rate changes.

Exchange rate €1 =	£0.50 £000s	£0.60 £000s	£0.80 £000s
French profit €28	14	17	22
Sterling profit	20	20	20
Operating profit	34	37	42
Interest on £175 @ 6%	11	11	11
Net profit	23	26	31

If for illustrative purposes all the group's borrowings are taken to be in Euros, the variation in reported profits with movement in exchange rates will be less even at a low interest rate of 3%. With a higher interest rate, the variation will be reduced still further.

Exchange rate €1 =	£0.50 £000s	£0.60 £000s	£0.80 £000s
Profit €28	14	17	22
Sterling profit	20	20	20
Operating profit	34	37	42
Interest on €292	4	5	7
Net profit	30	32	35

The net profit line in the above example shows that borrowing in a foreign currency where interest rates are low can have advantages. In the long run, experience suggests that it pays to borrow in more stable currencies where interest rates are lower, because the markets add a risk premium to interest rates in countries where inflation and political instability have been historically high. Most practitioners would submit that, to borrow in local currency, say in Turkey, where rates are well over 50% (at the time of writing), to match a Turkish investment would not make sense because the high interest rate would exceed the depreciation of the currency over time. It should be added that while this makes intuitive sense, and is borne out by observations of currencies in Latin America and Eastern Europe, there appears to be little empirical research on the subject.

In practice, it is rare for a company to borrow entirely in one currency. Practical considerations such as the costs associated with raising foreign currency debt may weigh with the parent. Another issue is the interest rate payable in each currency. If the group's objective is to match foreign currency profits with foreign currency interest payments, the movement of interest rates upwards or downwards would require a compensating adjustment in the amount borrowed. This is not efficient. A further point is the group's view of exchange rates in the medium term and its willingness to accept a degree of exposure to currency movements. Management will also need to consider management of the risk that arises when a translation exposure becomes a transaction exposure – that is to say, when an asset or company is sold. The exchange rate on the day will crystallise a foreign currency gain or a loss, and the extent of this gain or loss will be mitigated if there is a partial match through a foreign currency borrowing.

Covenants given to lenders in the group's loan documentation may be triggered

All bank and capital market loan documents will contain covenants designed to improve security and increase the lenders' chance of receiving repayment. The clauses most likely to be affected by foreign exchange movements are:

1. gearing, the ratio of debt to equity (adjusted share capital and reserves) will not be greater than a specified ratio, such as 100%;
2. interest cover, the borrower undertakes that pre-interest profits will exceed interest payments by a pre-determined factor, say two times or three times;
3. net worth, the borrower undertakes that its adjusted share capital and reserves will equal or be greater than an agreed figure.

The finance director of a company which has foreign currency assets will need to consider the effect of exchange rate movements on the group balance sheet and set the level of foreign currency debt accordingly. By way of example, take the case of Gander PLC's acquisition of GooseCo.

At the time of the acquisition, the sterling/Euro exchange rate was €1 = £0.60. Based on the balance sheet above, the Gander Group's gearing (the ratio of debt to equity) rose from 33% pre-acquisition to 95% financed entirely out of short-term loans. (Gearing only rises to 78% in the case where goodwill remains on the balance sheet, so companies should ensure in their bank documentation that goodwill is added back when the gearing ratio is calculated.) This level is high but it does not breach the 95% gearing limit that Gander's banks have requested should be incorporated into the documentation of a new 3-year multi-currency loan facility. The finance director realises that it may be possible for a 95% gearing covenant to be triggered by the movement in foreign exchange rates, so further analysis is called for.

Assuming that foreign currency assets and liabilities will be re-valued at year end exchange rates, Gander PLC's balance sheet will be as shown below if the rate stays at €1 = £0.60.

Gander PLC	Assets	Liabilities	€1 = £0.60
	£000s		
Sterling assets	300	75	Sterling debt
Euro assets	60	100	Euro debt
Goodwill	40	225	Equity
	400	400	(Gearing 78%)

On the basis of the above, the debt/equity ratio is 175/225 or 78% but it would be 175/185 or 95% if goodwill were written off to reserves. However, it is possible that the relative exchange rate could change from £0.60 to £0.50 or to £0.80. In the first case, the balance sheet would be as follows.

Gander PLC	Assets	Liabilities	€1 = £0.50
	£000s		
Sterling assets	300	75	Sterling debt
Euro assets	50	84	Euro debt
Goodwill	40	231	Equity
	390	390	(Gearing 69%)

At €1 = £0.50, the debt has fallen in sterling terms and equity has increased so the gearing is now 69%. (Note that it would be 83% if goodwill were written off to the reserves.)

The situation would worsen considerably if the Euro were to strengthen against sterling:

Gander PLC	Assets	Liabilities	€1 = £0.80
	£000s		
Sterling assets	300	75	Sterling debt
Euro assets	80	133	Euro debt
Goodwill	40	212	Equity
	420	420	(Gearing 98%)

At €1 = £0.80, the debt/equity ratio has risen to 98%. Under these circumstances, the company's bankers would be entitled to withdraw their funding.

Contrast the box above with the one below, where funding is entirely in sterling. Here the gearing falls if sterling depreciates against the French franc as follows:

Exchange rate €1 =	£0.50	£0.60	£0.80
		£000s	
Sterling assets	300	300	300
€100 assets	50	60	80
Goodwill	40	40	40
Total	390	400	420
Sterling debt	175	175	175
Equity	215	225	245
Gearing	81%	78%	71%

It can be seen from the above that reported profitability and debt levels shown in the accounts of the parent company and its group will be affected by changes in exchange rates (see Table 5.4). This in turn may lead to the triggering of financial covenants in documentation.

When considering which currency to choose for its liabilities, the finance director will need to consider all the above, together with the expected movement in interest rates in both currencies, the taxation of foreign currency gains and losses, and the accounting treatment.

With perfect foresight, the finance team can manage the currency of their debt so that gearing is minimised and profitability is maximised each year. There are few organisations that have the confidence or the will to risk the negative impact if such a policy goes badly wrong. Most organisations wishing to protect themselves against the effect of such changes will prefer to borrow in the currency of the acquired company to match the value of the assets, but in any case, only to the extent that the cash flows

Table 5.4 Summary of the effect of exchange rate changes

Reported effect of currency movements on	**Domestic currency weaker** **D F**	**Domestic currency stronger** **F D**
Overseas profits	Reported as improved	Reported as declined
Foreign currency interest	Reported as increased	Reported as lower
Foreign currency debt	Higher: Gearing worsens	Lower: Gearing improves
Domestic currency debt	Gearing improves	Gearing worsens
Equity	Increased	Decreased

from the company will repay the debt. This has sound commercial sense. If all else fails, expectations of the shareholders and analysts should be managed so that they can anticipate a variation in reported profits due to currency changes. The effect of currency movement on group profits does not then need to be actively managed.

Results from trading operations may be distorted

As set out above, it makes sense for an organisation partially or completely to match its foreign currency assets with foreign currency liabilities. These will both reduce the volatility of reported profits and protect it against excessive profits (which will probably fail to be taxed) on the sale of foreign currency assets.

The consequences of adopting a policy of matching will depend on the subsequent movement of exchange rates and the local accounting practices. The main areas of difference in accounting between jurisdictions are:

1 the extent to which matching is possible, i.e. whether realised or unrealised foreign exchange gains and losses can be offset;
2 when foreign exchange gains and losses are realised;
3 the rate used to translate foreign currency amounts, which may be historic, the closing rate for the period or the average rate for the period.

If a foreign currency loan is taken out to fund an equity investment or an asset purchase in foreign currency, the subsequent treatment of the loan and asset in the accounts will differ from jurisdiction to jurisdiction. The asset may be reported in the parent company's accounts at the original cost, while the loan may be revalued from year to year and the difference posted straight to reserves or through the profit and loss account.

The differences between accounting standards are particularly apparent when comparing the current UK and US GAAP. A set of British Airways accounts once actually listed 12 differences to explain the figures under the two sets of accounting rules. If a US airline buys an $100 million aircraft with dollar borrowings, there are no foreign exchange implications. For UK GAAP accounts, British Airways accounts for its aircraft purchases as though they were held in a foreign branch with dollar accounts. In a year when sterling depreciates against the dollar, the profits of British Airways will be considerably less when reported in US GAAP than they would be when reported under UK accounting rules, under which the gain on the value of the assets may be matched against the loss on the increase in the debt and exchange differences go to reserves.

If the finance director wants to ensure that the results from trading operations as shown in the local currency financial statements are not distorted, then the company will use matching rules if available and will partially or totally match foreign currency assets and liabilities.

Conclusion

International companies often have complex debt and equity structures. This chapter has taken a look at some of the reasons why such structures are established. It covers related financial issues such as methods of funding overseas assets, accounting and tax implications, with emphasis on problems that would be of relevance to the corporate treasurer.

The lesson is that, whereas general principles can be established, no project should be undertaken overseas unless the groundwork has been thoroughly investigated first. The rules are always changing and rarely do they get easier to understand. The key objective of an organisation is commercial success. All companies wish to avoid a situation where the tail is wagging the dog. There may be little point in establishing a sophisticated international corporate structure for tax or balance sheet purposes if the authorities can subsequently change the rules. This could leave the corporate group with a potential cost that far outweighs the original benefit and is more expensive to resolve or explain to shareholders and the investment community. The simplest arrangements are frequently the most effective, profitable and long lasting.

Case study: Parentco – the financing of foreign subsidiaries

Introduction

The practical issues outlined above regarding some of the additional complexities involved with the capitalising of a foreign subsidiary are now illustrated in two case studies. The first one involves the general financing of overseas subsidiaries following a major restructuring of the treasury organisation. The second involves a specific financing for the acquisition of an overseas company.

The company

This case study is based on the company, Parentco, first met in Chapter 3. This time the focus is on the financing of an overseas subsidiary, and the reader should reflect on the areas that were brought in for consideration in this specific case in addition to any issues that were important in the financing of the foreign operations as distinct from the domestic convertible bond.

The treasury risk management framework

Over the past few years, Parentco (the group) had undergone a fundamental change in both organisational structure and culture. These changes enabled the group treasury to overhaul the group's world-wide treasury function and secure an enhanced treasury risk management and control framework.

One of the many benefits of this re-engineering was that it enabled treasury to take a proactive support role with the operating units, which, through close contact and tangible results, supported the units in achieving their ambitious business goals. The financing of the overseas subsidiaries was a key driver in achieving this.

Management philosophy and general funding approach

The group's management philosophy was one of developing its five major global product groups on an international basis. This was considered to be best achieved by decentralising operating autonomy and accountability to the operating management. With regard to financing, however, this was a group treasury responsibility in order to achieve the most flexible and cost-effective financing for the group. Furthermore, any financing was undertaken on a legal entity basis and so would go across the product groups in a particular country.

With regard to the general funding approach, the group had clearly defined policies on interest coverage and debt/equity ratios, which were reviewed annually in the treasury operating plan. These ratios, managed on a consolidated group basis, give the treasury more flexibility in managing the financing structures of its overseas subsidiaries.

The majority of the financing for the group and its subsidiaries (of which there were more than 100) was undertaken in the name of the parent company with the group's major relationship banks. This financing, in the form of bilateral medium-term committed loan facilities, had an option to borrow in any currency (i.e. multicurrency) and could include any other nominated subsidiary. To ensure consistent treatment of all the major relationship banks, the main conditions (e.g. covenants, representation and warranties) contained in the documentation were the same. This form of financing instrument proved extremely versatile, as it enabled the company to have committed facilities available, but not necessarily drawn, while the group substantially streamlined and developed its operations.

Because over 50% of the group's revenues were derived in the US, the major borrower included in the committed facilities (other than the Parentco itself) was Group America, Inc. Essentially, substantially all US operating companies (OPCOs) formed part of the Group America, Inc consolidated legal entity. That and the fact that the cash concentration account structure operated in the US meant that the US holding company effectively funded the US OPCOs' requirements on an ongoing basis. The UK was similarly structured in that the UK OPCOs were normally part of the Parentco consolidated legal entity. Through this and the cash pooling in the UK, the Parentco effectively funded the daily requirements of the UK OPCOs.

The group's funding policy was to have committed facilities available of at least 130% of its anticipated peak borrowing requirements. While committed facilities form the majority of the facilities, Parentco also had a £80 million convertible bond (see Chapter 3). While the availability of ongoing committed funding is crucial, the group also considered the impact of the currency of funding for the management of the group's translation exposure. This was managed on a consolidated group basis with a view to protecting the group's gearing level (net debt to equity) from a material movement in currencies. This was reviewed on a regular basis and would be adjusted, from time to time, through the use of currency swaps.

While the majority of the group's funding was used to finance the UK and US OPCOs, more time-consuming and sometimes more challenging issues arose with the financing of the OPCOs based elsewhere. Group treasury negotiated this financing with the banks but were always sensitive to a number of issues, the most important of which was the actual requirement of the OPCO concerned.

Financing issues of operating companies

The key driver for the financing of overseas companies is that they must have sufficient availability of funds to meet their ongoing requirements at a competitive cost. Such financing must be structured so that it supports the commercial objectives of the specific business unit.

Over the past few years, businesses expanded into many new territories; these included South America, Continental and Eastern Europe, India and China. While each financing in itself may not be material from a group overall perspective, the issues and complexities of the many different markets require that these financings are considered on a case-by-case basis. Solutions have to be tailored for a specific set of circumstances.

While the facts may be different in each case, certain issues regularly arise that must be addressed. These include:

- the OPCOs' business requirements;
- identification of financing requirements;
- compliance with the group's treasury policy;
- source of funding;
- local balance sheet;
- tax considerations;
- political risk;
- cultural issues.

The OPCOs' business requirements

It is essential that any finance raised meets the business requirements of the OPCOs. Thus, group treasury must be aware of the underlying business plans of the company, whether it is a 100%-owned subsidiary, or a joint venture managed by Parentco, where the other partners have particular preferences. The country in which the company is located is also important, as this may influence the choice of banks to provide the funding. The key to making a success of any such financing is to work closely with the OPCO management (both locally and divisional) to understand their specific needs. Some of the countries into which the group expanded provided certain treasury challenges, which meant that operating management must also understand the overall group financing philosophy and approach, and the practical constraints that may arise by operating in different financial markets. As noted earlier, solutions must be tailored for a specific set of circumstances.

Identification of financing requirements

The identification of an OPCO's financing requirements should normally occur during the annual budget review process. Other circumstances do arise, for example, when a new acquisition has been arranged or additional capital expenditure has been approved.

Even where a further financial requirement has been identified, complications can arise, particularly if the OPCO is owned on a joint venture basis or, indeed, if the company is quoted on a local stock exchange. These situations tend to arise in the emerging markets and can take some time to resolve. In these circumstances, it was particularly helpful if the group could use the strength of one or more of the major relationship banks to provide support in the interim period.

Even if specific additional funding is not identified through the budget process, treasury must be cognisant of the overall financial health of the OPCOs. This is where close liaison with the Taxation Department is so essential, as these other circumstances can include:

- an OPCO with a negative net worth: this could give operating management some difficulty in its local market; this is normally easily resolved by injecting additional equity through new funds or the capitalisation or subordination of inter-group debt;
- the need to comply with local fiscal regulations (e.g. thin-capitalisation rules or time-barred utilisation of tax loss carry-forwards).

One issue that sometimes causes debates with operating management is the distinction between the availability of funds and cash balances. As a general treasury policy, the company aimed to reduce cash balances wherever possible. On some occasions, OPCO management may anticipate a capital expenditure and thus wish to retain cash locally. Under these circumstances, it is essential that treasury make them aware that it is the availability of funds (e.g. through local bank facilities) that is important, rather than the holding and building up of cash balances. In some countries, a cultural leap needs to be made by operating management, particularly where that company continues to be managed by its former owners.

Compliance with the group's treasury policy

Any financing, wherever undertaken, had to be approved by group treasury. Normally this meant that any documentation was reviewed by group treasury to ensure that it did not include covenants or other conditions that might jeopardise the local OPCO or, more importantly, conflict with covenants contained in the group's bilateral agreements with each of the major relationship banks.

Wherever possible, the company insisted on there being no covenants placed on the local OPCO. The purpose of this was to enable OPCO management to run their businesses as they saw fit without interference from the lender, but also to enable any legal entity to be structured in the most effective treasury and tax manner, particularly from a group perspective. In return for this flexibility and to achieve competitive pricing, some form of security may be required by the lending bank.

A further reason for treasury's involvement is that any financing had to be with an approved bank. Normally, this was either with one of the group's major relationship banks or with the domestic commercial bank, which had been selected during the banking review process. This is necessary as it helps limit the number of banks with which the group must deal but, perhaps more importantly, it means that the company could continue to consolidate the relationship with the banks who were then in a better position to support and service the OPCOs. Transactions can normally be completed quickly, and, if any misunderstandings arise, they may be promptly resolved. This is particularly significant where major relationship banks support OPCOs in emerging markets. The key element to enable this to happen is that there must be a strong and effective relationship and communication between the treasury and the bank.

In countries where OPCOs are starting for the first time, new banking relationships may have to be established and it is incumbent on the treasury to ensure they meet representatives from that bank (preferably locally, but also in London) to represent Parentco, and Parentco's banking approach, to that organisation. Establishing an effective relationship with a bank at an early stage is a powerful source of support, not only for the new OPCO, but also for future business units that establish themselves in that area later on.

Source of funding

As noted earlier, the source of funding for the UK and US holding companies was mainly by bilateral committed facilities with the group's major relationship banks. On a group basis, however, the international capital markets were constantly renewed and have, in the past, provided opportunities to raise funds through, for example, a convertible bond (see Chapter 3) or US private placement.

The source of funding for the other OPCOs, however, is normally one of the following:

- an intra-group loan;
- an injection of equity;
- capitalising of existing inter-company loan;
- arranging local bank overdraft or term loan finance.

The source of funding is determined by whether the OPCO needs further availability of cash, the term (short or long) of the requirement or whether the balance sheet needs restructuring.

Furthermore, the existing ownership structure must be considered. Most of the group's OPCOs were wholly owned, thus inter-group financing was normally the preferred route. However, the OPCOs had to establish different structures to support their local business objectives, which included wholly owned subsidiaries, joint ventures (independently managed or managed by a group company) or a shareholding in a public quoted company.

This ownership structure is relevant, particularly if it involves third parties (i.e. joint venture partnerships or individual [public] shareholders). For example, joint venture partners may well have their own preferred banking partners or, indeed, they may be constrained from injecting their agreed amount of equity into the partnership if they themselves are financially restricted. In these circumstances, it is essential that treasury work closely with OPCO management to develop pragmatic solutions. Where these situations arise, they can take time to develop and implement and can require patient managing.

Local balance sheet

Any financing must take into account the structure and strength of the local OPCO balance sheet. This is driven by the need to be in compliance with local fiscal and legal regulations as well as an awareness that the OPCO is competing in a particular market. A weak balance sheet may provide a commercial disadvantage to that company (e.g. suppliers not willing to provide on open credit terms). The translation exposure management of the local balance sheets was not undertaken on a company by company basis; this was managed on a consolidated group basis as discussed above.

Tax considerations

It is essential that any financing structure is efficient from a taxation standpoint, both local and group basis. This will differ from country to country, and each case must be reviewed on its merits. This close (and necessary) liaison between treasury and tax has already been covered.

Political risk

In developing its global product groups, the group invested in emerging markets. The potential for businesses is enormous but, in hand with that, there are associated political risks. This term can cover a multitude of issues including the appropriation of assets or the freezing of remittances being made outside the country. Even so, in the emerging markets, there seems to be a general easing of some of the political risks as governments become increasingly more aware of the potential benefits that inward investment may bring to their country. Political risk, however, is still a major commercial consideration when investing overseas. Depending on the particular country, the company might have involved one of the major relationship banks in any financing or, indeed raise funding from an indigenous bank. In either case, the company discussed with the banks the purpose of the proposed action, to ensure they were fully aware of the commercial and financial objectives. The cost of any stand-alone financing in some of these territories can be high; to minimise this cost where possible, some form of support may have to be provided.

One of the considerations in obtaining bank finance, however, is that, should political risk arise in a particular country, action by the government against the local branch of an international bank is less likely to be taken than against a foreign-owned OPCO. Political risk can also encompass restrictions on the payment of interest and dividends or even trading balances if the funds flow outside the country. While this is sometimes temporary, it is inconvenient and requires careful handling and close communication with the local OPCO.

Political risk is also an area where close and effective banking relationships can provide significant advantages. Banks themselves have to consider their exposure to emerging markets and, within these, specific country risk. This means that there may be a limited amount of lending availability by a bank for a particular country; the bank would normally allocate that to its major relationship customers. The margin charged by the bank will, in some respect, reflect their perceived risk profile of a particular country.

Cultural issues

A major consideration in the financing of overseas OPCOs is the need to be aware of, and sensitive to, the different banking structures, approaches, practices and cultures that arise in each country. Thus, banking and funding practices are very different in the US or Italy, India or China and must be taken into account when dealing with the local institutions. If an overseas business manager fails to recognise and act on this, it could have a negative impact on the business. Treasury can play a key role in managing, and indeed resolving, any difficulties that might arise in these circumstances.

Conclusion

The key driver in the financing of overseas subsidiaries is to ensure that each OPCO has the funding it needs to continue its business operations. Each situation should be considered on a case-by-case basis, and tailor-made solutions agreed with each OPCO management. A number of issues when considering and raising finance have been discussed; these will, of course, be different in each case.

Other corporates may face some of the same issues discussed or, indeed, other issues. The issues covered above are not exhaustive but are intended to give the reader an insight into the many challenges facing treasury as it supports the operating units in achieving their business objectives.

Case study: Financing the acquisition of Dr Pepper/Seven-Up

Introduction

In this case study, the financing needed for a specific overseas acquisition is examined. It is interesting to see how the company focused on two main objectives, those of enhancing EPS and on the ultimate credit rating and, importantly, how it balanced these two potentially conflicting objectives. Other criteria are also brought into what is essentially a balancing act.

Background

Cadbury Schweppes had been courting the American soft drinks company, Dr Pepper/Seven-Up (DPSU), since 1986. The knot was finally tied in January 1995 when Cadbury Schweppes agreed to pay $1.7 billion in cash to acquire the 78% of the equity it did not already own.

How much to pay?

Over those 9 years, Cadbury Schweppes (CS) progressively expanded its soft drinks business in the US (see Table 5.5), but were still only the fourth largest player in the soft drinks market.

Table 5.5 Cadbury Schweppes' expansion in US soft drinks

1986	Acquired Canada Dry for $140 million
1986	First stake in Dr Pepper
1989	Acquired Crush (orange soda) for $220 million
1993	Increased stake in Dr Pepper/Seven-Up
1993	Acquired A&W Brands (root beer) for $334 million

Table 5.6 History of DPSU and Cadbury Schweppes

1984	First leveraged buy-out of Dr Pepper
1986	Second leveraged buy-out of Dr Pepper: CS bought 30% for $18 million
1986	First leveraged buy-out of Seven-Up and management agreement with Dr Pepper
1987	CS bought 4% of Dr Pepper for $3 million
1988	Third leveraged buy-out and merger with Seven-Up. CS received $90 million cash, $18 million in DPSU securities and 8% of the new company's equity
1989	CS received $9 million cash from redemption of bridge notes
1993	Initial Public Offering of equity to raise $305 million. CS received $18 million cash from redemption of Preferred Stock. Equity stake diluted to 6%
1993	CS purchased 20% of the equity for $231 million
1995	CS purchased the remaining 74% of the equity plus the outstanding options for $1.7 billion

DPSU, at number 3, was twice as big as our US business and Dr Pepper was the fastest growing brand in the market, which is otherwise dominated by The Coca-Cola Company and PepsiCo Inc. DPSU, meanwhile, had gone through three successive leveraged buy-outs, followed in 1993 by an Initial Public Offering of its equity (see Table 5.6). The business had grown more valuable as its prodigious cash flow paid down its debt. In 1986, when CS paid $17.5 million for 30%, the company's equity was valued at $58 million compared with $2.2 billion in 1995.

To be a serious player in the world's carbonated soft drinks market, we knew that we must achieve critical mass in the US. The only realistic way of doing that was to acquire DPSU. The dice were not all loaded in DPSU's favour, however. Their share price had risen on the back of takeover speculation and many of the shareholders wanted to realise this value sooner rather than later. Barring acquisition by a new entrant to the industry, we were the most obvious acquiror, as Coca-Cola and PepsiCo faced serious problems on anti-trust grounds (PepsiCo owns the Seven-Up brand outside the US but was prevented by the Federal Trade Commission (FTC) from acquiring the brand in the US in 1986, so it went to a leveraged buy-out and subsequently merged with Dr Pepper, which Coca-Cola had also been prevented from buying by the FTC) and nobody else had the necessary financial muscle readily available.

How to finance?

Having decided how much we were prepared to pay (by discounting expected future cash flows), the financing structure was determined by balancing a number of objectives, of which the two principal ones were:

- the deal had to enhance earnings per share in 1996 and beyond with no significant dilution in 1995;

- we were not prepared to accept more than a one-notch downgrade in our long-term credit rating, i.e. from A1/A+ to A2/A for senior debt.

These were potentially in conflict with each other: too much equity and we would fail on the first; and we would be downgraded more heavily if we had too much debt.

Our modelling of different ratios of debt and equity in the financing structure soon revealed that we could not satisfy both objectives with pure debt and equity alone. We found that we needed something that combined some of the features of both, namely around £200 million of perpetual quasi-equity. This would not enhance our fixed charge coverage ratio (see Fig. 5.4 for definition), which we consider more important than interest coverage as it takes account of the servicing costs of all forms of non-equity finance. However, it would give comfort to the rating agencies by improving our ability to repay our debt (as measured by the cash flow/borrowings ratio). Pure equity (£500 million from a rights issue of ordinary shares) was required with the balance of funding coming from a newly arranged bank facility.

We would be taking on around £1 billion of additional debt (including DPSU's existing debt). As Table 5.7 shows, this would have a dramatic effect on our balance sheet gearing. To explain the accounting policies behind our balance sheet at the time (e.g. goodwill arising on acquisitions written-off to reserves; acquired brands capitalised but not home grown ones) is beyond the scope of the case study. Suffice to say that they rendered the gearing ratio meaningless.

Coverage ratios

We had, therefore, for many years sought to focus the attention of our shareholders, banks and rating agencies towards the fixed charge coverage ratio as a more meaningful indicator of our financial gearing. We had stated publicly on numerous occasions that we would not wish this ratio to fall much below four times for any significant period of time. This was consistent with the one-notch rating downgrade that we were prepared to accept. We were therefore confident that all observers would regard the gearing level as

Trading profit + Dividends from associates + $\frac{1}{3}$ operating lease rentals

divided by

Net interest charge + Preference dividends + $\frac{1}{3}$ operating lease rentals

5.4 Definition of fixed-charge cover.

Table 5.7 Profit and loss account and balance sheet for 1994

Pro-forma consolidated profit and loss account for 1994

	CS (£m)	DPSU (£m)	Acquisition financing and adjustments (£m)	Pro-forma (£m)
Sales	4030	503		4533
Operating profit	521	133	9	663
Interest	(42)	(53)	(32)	(127)
Profit before tax	479	80	(23)	536
Tax	(155)	(29)	17	(167)
Minority interests: equity	(54)	–	–	(54)
non-equity	–	–	(16)	(16)
Preference dividends	(8)	–	–	(8)
Net income	**262**	**51**	**(22)**	**291**
Interest coverage ratio	12.0	2.5		5.1
Fixed charge cover ratio	8.0	2.5		4.0

Pro-forma consolidated balance sheet for 1994

	CS (£m)	DPSU (£m)	Acquisition financing and adjustments (£m)	Pro-forma (£m)
Tangible fixed assets	1346	12	–	1358
Intangibles (i.e. brands)	522	264	883	1669
Investments	200	–	(150)	50
Working capital	(90)	10	16	(64)
	1978	**286**	**749**	**3013**
Ordinary share capital and reserves	1319	(219)	45	1145
Preference shares	180	–	–	180
Minority interests: equity	128	–	–	128
non-equity	–	–	191	191
Net borrowings	351	505	513	1369
	1978	**286**	**749**	**3013**
Gearing ratio	24%	NA		108%

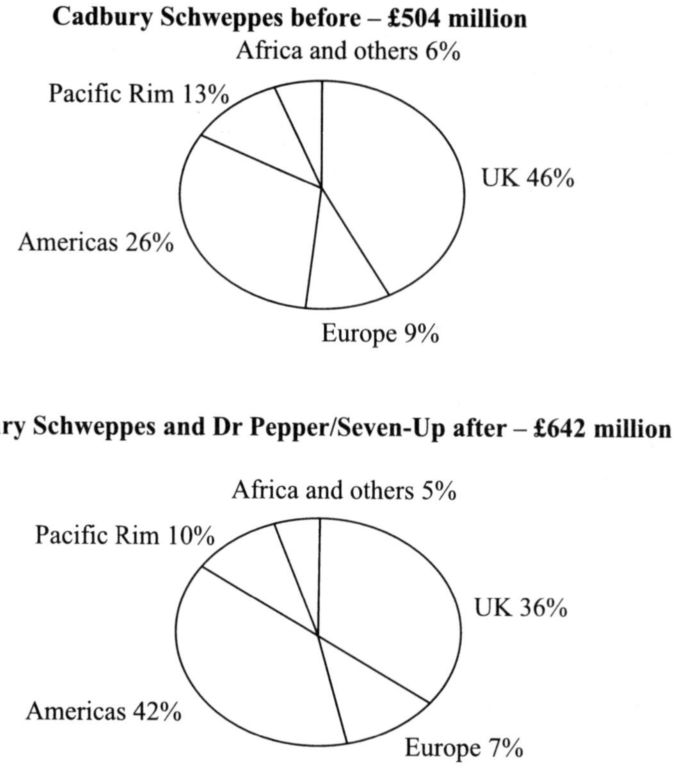

5.5 Cadbury Schweppes before and Cadbury Schweppes and Dr Pepper/Seven-Up after the acquisition.

acceptable, even though our credit ratings were unlikely to be raised again for two or three years.

The acquisition would increase the proportion of our overseas earnings to around two-thirds (see Fig. 5.5), while the rights issue would create increased dividend obligations for the future.

We expected that we would not be able to recover all of our Advance Corporation Tax (ACT; now abolished) – a payment of a proportion of mainline corporation tax, payable when a dividend is distributed, in advance of the normal payment date of the tax due, in the future and investigated the possibility of structuring the acquisition financing to mitigate this problem. A common approach to surplus ACT problems in those days was the enhanced scrip dividend (ESD), but these were disliked by institutional shareholders on the grounds of being disguised rights issues. But what if we used one as a rights issue? Well, it seemed illogical to be asking our shareholders to subscribe to a rights issue and then be paying them a substantial dividend a couple of months later. A second interim dividend with an ESD alternative was therefore announced, in lieu of the final dividend, at the time of the announcement of the rights issue.

ESD and share price

Under a traditional ESD, the number of shares to be issued is determined by the market price of the shares at the end of the ESD election period. There was a risk that our share price would fall substantially once the deal was announced, which would lead to more shares than planned being issued. Equally, if we fixed the number of shares to be issued at the outset and the price fell, there would be no incentive for shareholders to take up the ESD. The eventual solution to this conundrum was to fix the number of shares to be issued and underwrite the minimum price at which shareholders could sell them (at the same price as the rights issue). Our advisoers were, of course, willing to do the underwriting for a suitably (im)modest fee! Thus was born the UESDA, or underwritten enhanced scrip dividend alternative (see Appendix 5.1).

UESDSA

The UESDA would effectively raise about £100 million (by avoiding cash outflow on dividend payments), leaving £400 million to be raised by the rights issue. For this, we adopted a 'trombone' structure, whereby only part of the equity is raised initially, the balance being called once the acquisition has been declared unconditional. There were risks (though we considered them small) that the acquisition would be blocked on anti-trust grounds or that a competing bidder would emerge. In addition, we wanted to avoid the risk of severe earnings dilution if we raised all the equity and then the deal failed to complete. Discussions between our advisers and the Stock Exchange resulted in our being able to call only 30% of the rights issue in the first tranche as compared with the more normal 50%.

Preferred securities

The quasi-equity was to be preferred securities of the style first issued by Grand Metropolitan in late 1994. The principal features of these are set out in Appendix 5.2 and $400 million were successfully issued at the beginning of April. This was increased from our original target of $300 million (i.e. approximately £200 million equivalent) because of the strength of the market.

New debt

Table 5.8 shows that the final, though largest, piece of the financing jigsaw was to be new debt. The facility to be arranged, at $2400 million, was larger than the acquisition consideration, as it also had to cover refinancing of DPSU's own bank debt, bridging finance until the cash from the second

Table 5.8 Funding requirement

	$m
Funding requirement	
Consideration	1700
DPSU debt to be retained (discount notes)	250
DPSU debt to be refinanced	550
	2500
	$m
Funding structure	
Rights issue of ordinary shares (£395 m)	630
UESDA	140
Preferred securities	300
DPSU discount notes	250
New bank debt	1180
	2500

tranche of the rights issue and the preferred securities was received, and a top-up to our existing facilities to satisfy Stock Exchange requirements that we had sufficient facilities to meet our needs over the next 18 months or so.

Short-run versus long-run costs

In structuring the facilities, we wanted to minimise the running cost, i.e. the commitment fees. This was more important than the margin, as we did not intend to borrow on the facility for long, but to use it to back-up commercial paper and other cheaper funding sources. We also intended, long-term, to take funding from the bond markets, so we expected to cancel a large part of the facility within the first year. Recognising this, we adopted a '364 day plus term-out option' for $1.4 billion of the facilities. Under this option, the commitment period is 364 days, but any outstandings at the end of that period convert automatically into a term loan, which can run for up to a further 2 years and can be prepaid at any time but not redrawn. This effectively gave us the 3-year commitment we wanted, but without the capital adequacy costs normally associated with it (see Appendix 5.3 for further details).

The group of banks

We are strong believers in the virtues of relationship banking and so decided from the outset that we wanted this facility to be provided by our existing principal banks and, as far as possible, to be on the same terms as our existing facilities. We felt that a group of eight banks was about right and drew up our target list. We identified that we wanted one bank to act as a coordinator during the negotiations and also as the agent bank. Accordingly, in mid-January, when we could see that negotiations with DPSU were progressing well, we talked confidentially to our chosen lead bank. They soon warmed to the task of leading the facility.

On Wednesday 18 January, a bank that was not in our target group of eight came to see us. They said that, if we were to acquire DPSU, they would be willing to underwrite the bank finance jointly with one other bank. This was an attractive proposition as we could, at that time, see that the period between approaching the eight banks and signing the deal was likely to be compressed owing to US regulatory requirements to announce the acquisition as quickly as possible once outline agreements had been reached. The pricing quoted by this bank was significantly higher than we had expected, so we decided to sit on the offer until the Friday when our chosen lead bank was due to present its pricing.

We then asked how they would feel about joint underwriting with another bank and they said that they would be proposing this on the Friday also. When they gave us their pricing, it was almost exactly in line with our expectations. We took the immediate decision to approach a third bank (one of our original eight) and at 4.45 p.m. rang the London office of a North American bank. We had had discussions about 'substantial' acquisition finance over many years, although the figures had never reached the $1200 million commitment we were now proposing. Punctuated by comments like 'it's a big number . . .', they decided to come and see us and an hour later were in our offices, having already discussed the proposal with their head office. They worked through the weekend, gave us pricing proposals, which were close to our expectations, on the Sunday and had credit approval from Head Office by 4.30 p.m. on the Monday (11.30 a.m. local time in the Head Office) – an astonishing achievement.

The launch

That Sunday lunchtime, our project team met in the boardroom, surrounded by the Sunday papers proclaiming that we were about to announce the acquisition of DPSU. We knew that we would have to make an announcement to the Stock Exchange the following day, but although we expected to reach agreement with DPSU in a matter of days, we were not yet able to give any details as negotiations were incomplete. We also knew that simply announcing that we were 'in discussion' with DPSU would probably send our share price down with consequent effects on the pricing of the rights issue and the whole financing structure. In consultation with our advisers, we decided to announce that we were in discussions but that we would only enter into the transaction if its impact would be broadly neutral on EPS in 1995 and enhancing thereafter, would not take our interest coverage below 4.5 times, and that the rights issue would raise about £500 million. We felt that our share price would probably fall immediately, as the market's fear of a major acquisition was confirmed as highly likely, and then pull back as investors realised that the rights issue would not be as heavy as many had feared. We were proved right – it fell 12 p on announcement and then recovered most of it by the time we priced the rights issue 3 days later.

We spent those 3 days simultaneously negotiating the acquisition agreement with DPSU, the bank facility, the rights issue and UESDA with our investment bank and briefing the rating agencies. We finally signed all the documents at about 6 a.m. on Thursday 26 January and announced the transaction before the opening of the London stock market.

Conclusion

Subsequently, we put the financing onto a more permanent basis by sub-underwriting the bank facility to an additional 11 banks and then issuing the preferred securities. By mid-April our credit ratings had been confirmed with a one-notch downgrade (short-term ratings remained at A-1/P-1) and we had stopped borrowing on the bank facility, switching to the cheaper commercial paper markets and just using the banks to provide long-term back-up liquidity. Then in September, we tapped the Eurobond market for $300 million of 4-year money followed by a 5-year £150 million bond in October and a 3-year $200 million one in November. These extended the maturity profile of our debt and ensured that we could cancel the '364 day plus term-out' part of the facility before the first anniversary, when we would have had to draw it down to ensure its continued availability.

The acquisition of DPSU was the biggest strategic move that Cadbury Schweppes had made since the merger that created it in 1969. It changed the shape of the business with almost two-thirds of profits generated overseas, and the Americas contributing more than the company's UK home base. It changed the group's financial profile too with 12% more sales, 27% more operating profit and debt almost quadrupled.

Appendix 5.1: The underwritten enhanced scrip dividend alternative

On 26 January 1995, a dividend of 11 p per ordinary share was declared. As an alternative, shareholders could elect to receive 0.0432432 of a new ordinary share for each ordinary share they held.

Our broker made an offer to ordinary shareholders to sell the shares thus acquired at a price of not less than £3.40 per share. At this underwritten price, shareholders would receive approximately 14.7 p per share, representing a 34% increment over the declared cash dividend.

When the election period for the UESDA and the underwritten sale offer closed, shares were sold in the open market at a net price of £4.221. Thus, ordinary shareholders who had elected to receive the scrip dividend and then sell their shares received approximately 18.3 p per share, representing a 66% increment over the declared cash dividend.

The holders of 88% of ordinary shares elected to receive the ESD and thus the company avoided a cash outflow of £81 million in dividend and £20 million in associated ACT.

Appendix 5.2: Preferred securities

Issued by:	Cadbury Schweppes Delaware L.P.
Guaranteed by:	Cadbury Schweppes PLC
Dividend:	8.625% paid quarterly
Term:	Perpetual, but with an issuer call option at any time after 7 years
Purchasers:	Mostly US retail investors
Investor tax treatment:	Taxable income from a limited partnership
Issuer tax treatment:	By passing the issue proceeds back to CS PLC as Capital Interests (purchased by the Delaware limited partnership), CS PLC is able to obtain a UK tax deduction on payments made on the Capital Interests (which are equal to the preferred securities dividends)
Accounting treatment:	The preferred securities and the dividends thereon are treated as non-equity minority interests in the balance sheet and in the profit and loss account

Appendix 5.3: Principal terms of the bank facilities

Facility A:	$1 billion revolving credit facility incorporating swingline option for $500 million
Facility B:	$1.4 billion revolving credit facility converting to term loan after 364 days
Term:	3 years
Covenants:	Negative pledge *Pari passu* Material adverse change Cross default
Financial:	Consolidated total borrowings not to exceed 1.5 times adjusted consolidated net worth at any year end
Margin:	22.5 basis points
Commitment fee on undrawn amounts:	Facility A, 10 basis points Facility B, 6.25 basis points

Chapter

6 Dividends

Introduction

Shareholders obtain their return from a company in two ways, namely, through an increase in share value and through dividend flow. Since the increase in share value is simply a reflection of future growth in dividend flows, one can effectively argue that share price reflects the net present value of future expected dividend flows (the terminal value of the share on selling will reflect future expected cash flows from that date). The dividend flows will be discounted at the correct cost of equity capital for the risk involved.

The theory

As with the debt equity decision itself, there is a discussion about whether or not dividend policy can affect the value of the company. If it cannot, then the dividend decision would not be that important in the capital structure decision. If, on the other hand, it can be seen that the dividend policy of a company affects the value of equity, then this would have a bearing on the amount of equity in the balance sheet and, hence, have an impact on the capital structure decision. Again, there are theoretical and practical aspects to this debate, so let us start with the theoretical background before seeing how life's imperfections are able to spoil a perfect theory.

The theoretical stance is that the way, or indeed whether, a dividend is paid will not affect the overall value to the shareholder, and the dividend decision is therefore a residual one. In other words, the theory maintains that the company is faced with an array of investment opportunities, and the company should take up all suitable investments that give the shareholder the required rate of return. Any retained earnings available after financing those investments should be returned to the shareholders for them to do with as they please. The dividend decision thus becomes a residual decision after all financing has been completed.

The shareholders, it is argued, should be indifferent between seeing their money earn a suitable rate of return in the company or utilising it themselves. If the dividend is retained in this way, the value of it will be reflected in the share value. In a perfect capital market, if dividends are not paid out and cash is needed by the shareholders, they are able to sell their shares and raise cash. Because shareholders are able to raise cash in this way themselves, they would be unwilling to impute any extra value to a company that pays out a cash dividend.

Miller and Modigliani (1961) produced a proof of the irrelevance of dividends as follows: the present value of a share will equal the dividend flow plus the terminal value of the share at the end of the year, discounted at the correct cost of capital.

$$PVS_0 = \frac{(D_1 + P_1)}{1 + r} \qquad [6.1]$$

where PVS_0 is the present value of a share today, or today's share price, D_1 is the expected dividend at year end, P_1 is the terminal value of share at year end, and $1 + r$ is the company's risk-adjusted cost of capital.

The total value of the company will therefore equal today's share price times the number of shares in issue (N), or $NPVS_0$, which is the present value of the total dividend issued at the year end plus the total value of stock outstanding at year end but minus any stock issued in the meantime (M). This may be described as follows:

$$NPVS_0 = \frac{[ND_1 + (N + M)P_1 - MP_1]}{1 + r} \qquad [6.2]$$

The amount of stock issued in the meantime will depend on the amount of investment (I) that takes place in the period less any earnings (E) for the period but plus any dividend paid out from those earnings. For example, if investment opportunities total £1 million and earnings for the period are £1 million but a cash dividend of £500 000 is paid out, then new stock (assuming no debt is being used) to the value of £500 000 must be issued. Thus, the value of new stock (MP_1) at the year end will equal to:

$$MP = I - (E - ND_1) \qquad [6.3]$$

If we now substitute this term for MP_1 in equation (6.2), we obtain equation (6.4).

$$NPVS_0 = \frac{[ND_1 + (N + M)P_1 - \{I - (E - ND_1)\}]}{1 + r} \qquad [6.4]$$

The two ND_1 terms cancel out, leaving equation [6.5], giving the value of the firm, but with no term for a dividend, i.e. it is independent of the dividend level:

$$NPVS_0 = \frac{[(N = M)P_1 - I + E]}{1 + r} \qquad [6.5]$$

If a dividend distribution were made, the value of that distribution to shareholders in terms of pounds in their pockets, would be immediately offset by an equivalent drop in share price. This is easily illustrated with a simple numerical example.

Suppose we have a company, Divco, which at the start of the year has net assets of £3 million and 1 000 000 issued shares. During the year Divco earns £300 000. At the end of the year, net assets will have risen to £3 300 000. If Divco retains the earnings, the share value will be:

$$\frac{£3\,300\,000}{1\,000\,000} \text{ or } £3.30 \text{ per share}$$

If, on the other hand, Divco decides to distribute the earnings, then each shareholder will receive

$$\frac{£300\,000}{1\,000\,000} = £0.30$$

The net asset value of the company will be £3 million so each share is valued at:

$$\frac{£3\,000\,000}{1\,000\,000} = £3.00$$

Therefore, the total value to the shareholder is £3.30.

We could complicate life a little by presenting Divco with an investment opportunity costing £300 000, which gives an NPV of zero (i.e. giving exactly the required rate of return).

Divco balance sheet pre-distribution

	£		£
Retained earnings (cash)	300 000	Debt	0
Other assets	3 000 000	Equity (1 million shares)	3 300 000
NPV new investment	0		
Total assets	3 300 000	Total value	3 300 000
		Per shareholder	3.30

If a cash distribution is made of £300 000, then the company value will drop to £3 000 000 and the per share value to £3.00. Since £300 000 is needed, 100 000 new shares will be issued at £3.00.

Divco balance sheet post-distribution

	£		£
Assets (inc. new inv.)	3 300 000	Debt	0
NPV new investment	0	Equity	3 300 000
Total assets	3 300 000	Total value (1 100 000 shares)	3 300 000
		Per share value	3.00

It can be seen that 30p per share of value has been lost to the old shareholders and transferred to the 1 000 000 new shareholders. This loss is exactly offset, of course, by the 30p dividend per share that the old shareholders received.

Imperfections

Modigliani and Miller's proof was based on a perfect capital market. This was previously discussed in Chapter 1 but, briefly, this involves no taxes, no transaction costs, information is free and uniformly distributed, and shares are divisible. As these have already been dealt with, we shall not deal with them all in detail again but focus on tax.

Tax

As it is clear that capital markets are not perfect, we now need to focus on the effect that introducing imperfections will have on the dividend decision. A major issue to tackle is the one concerning taxes. Where there is a difference between income tax and capital gains tax, then there may be value added by a company pursuing a particular dividend policy. Suppose income tax is at 40% and capital gains tax is at 30%. If we were a shareholder of Divco holding 10% of the shares, we could expect an income of £30 000 if the £300 000 of earnings is distributed.

Shareholder's position

Owns 100 000 shares (bought at £3.00per share)

	£
Value (if earnings distributed)	300 000
Income	30 000
Tax @ 40%	12 000
Net dividend received	18 000

Suppose the dividend is retained, but that the shareholder needs an income of £18 000 and decides to create a dividend by selling shares.

Owns 100 000 shares
Value if earnings not distributed £330 000
Value per share £3.30

On every share sold at £3.30, there will be capital gains paid on 30p at 30%, or 9p per share. Therefore, the shareholder will receive a net amount of £3.21 per share.

To raise £18 000, the shareholder must sell £18 000/3.21 or 5607.4766 shares.

		£
Amount raised 5607.4766 × £3.30	=	18 505
Initial cost 5607.4766 × £3.00	=	16 822
Capital gain		1 682
Tax at 30%		505
Net receipt		18 000

Net benefit to shareholder

	£
Investment remaining of 94 392.5234 shares @ £3.30	311 495
Versus original	300 000
Difference	11 495

This is the difference between the income tax of £12 000 and the capital gains tax of £505.

To an extent, this calculation masks the tax effect, since the shareholder has only sold a small proportion of the shares and therefore left a large proportion of the capital gain unrealised and therefore untaxed. As well as having a lower tax rate on manufactured dividend, the shareholder has, however, rolled forward any tax due on the shares unsold until the gains are realised, and this does have a beneficial effect in terms of present values.

Transaction costs

While the above illustrates the tax advantage to the shareholders of different 'dividend' policies, it has ignored a few issues. The first is that of transaction costs. Obviously, there are transaction costs, and these must be taken into account. If in this instance transaction costs equalled 0.5%, this would mean selling 5627.7259 shares (see Appendix 6.1), or roughly 20 more shares. For many, especially those with small shareholdings, these transaction costs can become significant. The second issue concerns the divisibility of shares. The calculation says that we need to sell 5627.7259 shares. In reality, we cannot divide up shares in this way, so it is unlikely that a shareholder would be able to quite duplicate a dividend pay-out. This is not a major issue where share prices are relatively low, but may become more important where share prices are large, e.g. hundreds of pounds or thousands of dollars per share.

Dilution effect

One issue that may be a major one is the dilution effect. In the first example, the shareholder held 10% of the shares, and this was reduced to approximately 9.4%. There may well be reasons why shareholders do not wish to have their holdings reduced. Issues of control are obvious, as are problems with index-tracking investment funds, where certain proportions of particular shares must be held for weighting purposes but where income is needed nonetheless.

Three points of view

So far, we have looked at what Brealey and Myers (1970) would call 'the middle of the road' party, who feel that dividend policy does not influence share value. We have also looked at tax and transaction issues, but, if tax rates were broadly in line, there should be little advantage in one or another policy (high pay-out, low pay-out). We need to consider briefly two other groups, which are (as Brealey and Myers put it) the Leftists and the Rightists.

The Leftists would argue that, except for a residual policy, i.e. only paying out earnings surplus to current and foreseeable investment needs, paying out dividends would be positively harmful to share value if retained earnings are needed for investment. This is because the company would have to go to the trouble and expense of raising new debt and equity. There would be a loss of value to shareholders to receive a dividend (taxed) and to replace the needed funds with a new equity issue, issued at a discount and with large flotation costs, or with debt, again with issue costs.

The Rightists, on the other hand, argue for an increase in share value with a high pay-out ratio. Their argument is probably based more on the psychological aspects of dividend policy than anything else. There are two aspects to this. One is the safety argument, that at least the dividend paid is cash in hand, whereas if left in the company it is left at risk. However, if the dividend paid out is not needed for consumption, then the investor will probably reinvest in an investment of a similar class of risk anyway.

Clientele effect

When we examined the issue previously, we saw that whether the shareholder has cash or a higher share price, they should be indifferent between the two, but in fact may not be. This gives rise to the potential for clientele effects, i.e. there are classes of shareholder who need a dividend stream as income. Widows and orphans are often put into this category and so are some investment and pension funds. A high pay-out ratio will appeal to those clients and thus cause a demand by them for the shares. This hopefully will be reflected in a higher share price. Similarly, a low pay-out policy could be aimed at a high-tax-bracket client. The overall market should reflect a balance between these client groups and the companies targeting them. Unless there is unsatisfied demand for a particular policy, it would be difficult for a company to affect its share price in this way.

Information effect

The other aspect is that there may be an informational side to dividend policy. Shareholders do not have as much information as managers do about the performance and prospects of a company. They are, therefore, always looking for clues to increase their knowledge. Now you could argue that managers spend a lot of time telling shareholders what the prospects are and therefore the future should already be reflected in the share price. While this is undoubtedly true (except for companies where the management is currently uncommunicative), nonetheless, there is nothing like putting your money where your mouth is. Given that the shareholders have faith in the management, and given that management do not like to announce dividend cuts, an announcement of a dividend increase will indicate to the market that the management has confidence that the dividend will be maintained in the future, and that the prospects for growth are good. Because of this news, investors will buy the stock and the share price will go up. A reading of the financial press will certainly back up this view, whether or not it can be 'logically' supported, given the foregoing arguments.

Empirical evidence on dividends

Management attitudes

In his 1956 study, Lintner interviewed a number of financial managers concerning their dividend policies and found four common themes. He found that:

1 managers believe that firms should have a target long-term pay-out ratio;
2 in setting dividends, rather than focus on the absolute level, they focus more on the change in pay-out;
3 dividends would be changed if there were a major unanticipated and permanent change in earnings; and, following from this;
4 managers try to avoid dividend increases that may have to be reversed.

Tax influences

Elton and Gruber (1970) found some evidence of a tax effect in their ex-dividend day test. They discovered that the price of a share dropped by less than the amount of the declared dividend when the share went ex-dividend, i.e. when the purchaser of the share would not receive the dividend due on that share. To put it another way, the seller of the share keeps the right to receive the dividend. They discovered that, rather than drop by the amount of the dividend, the price dropped by, on average, 78% of the dividend. Appendix 6.2 illustrates why this might happen.

High pay-out, high returns

Another area that has been examined is the effect of dividend pay-out on stock prices. If, as the Rightists claim, a high dividend pay-out is a good thing, we would expect to see, overall, higher stock returns for high pay-out stocks as the demand for the stock pushes its price up, giving extra return to existing shareholders. In 1974, Black and Scholes drew the conclusion that 'it is not possible to demonstrate that the expected returns on high yield stocks differ from the expected returns on low yield stocks either before or after taxes'. However, Rosenberg and Marathe (1978) did find a positive relationship between dividend yields and stock returns. Litzenberger and Ramaswamy (1982) concluded that 'the data indicate that there is a positive but non-linear association between common stock returns and dividend yields'.

Signalling

A number of studies have examined the signalling effect of dividends. Ross (1977) found that unanticipated changes in dividends were interpreted by the market as signals. Litzenberger and Ramaswamy, in contrast, said that 'the conclusion of the present study is that these significant yield effects can not be pinned to the information content in the prior knowledge that the firm will declare a dividend of unknown magnitude'. They draw this conclusion based on their study, which used information that would have been available to the investor already. Therefore, the dividend announcement would not convey any new information.

Miller and Rock (1985), however, state that 'such price responses (to dividend announcements) have always been part of the real world folklore, but only recently has their presence been demonstrated convincingly', and they conclude that these dividend announcement effects demonstrate the asymmetry of information that exists between shareholders and managers. They also discuss in this paper whether this information effect can be manipulated by managers to give wrong, and over-optimistic, signals to the market. This might cause a short-term rise in share prices until, of course, they fail to deliver. While shares would return to their 'correct' level, there is a chance that those who sold their share at the peak will make profits at the expense of new entrants or those that held on to their shares. Market discipline and rules on insider trading go some way towards controlling this, as does market awareness that this might happen, and hence will be discounted into the share price.

Perhaps the last word should go to Marsh and Merton (1987), who say 'in summary, there are a number of conflicting theories of dividend behaviour and the empirical studies to date provide little compelling evidence for one over the others'. They themselves find evidence only of a mild information effect and that real dividend changes are driven by a lagged effect of real share price changes.

Summary of the theory

If the 'middle of the roaders' are correct, then, from an overall value perspective, the dividend decision is not an important one. However, there do appear, in spite of mixed empirical evidence, to be issues involved with tax and information effects. How important the tax effects are will depend on how far apart different tax rates are. The tax rates of the individual investor will also only be of any importance if the management of a company pay any attention to them. It would be legitimate for the management simply to declare a dividend policy and then let the clients select themselves and arrange their own tax affairs to maximise their own returns. It does seem clear though that, once a management has declared a dividend policy, it should maintain it, or at least give good warning and a good explanation of any changes.

Practicalities

Managers will have to pay attention to certain practical issues such as the legal requirements in setting the dividend, restrictive covenants and company-based tax issue. In addition to these, we might expect financial managers to have an eye on the financial realities of life, such as cash flows, investment requirements, stability of earnings and growth.

There are a range of possible dividend policies (no dividend, residual, constant and special dividends), and which a company chooses will depend upon the company circumstances and the objectives of the management.

No dividend

The no dividend policy may be found in a company that is fast growing and needs every drop of cash that it is able to lay its hands on to finance that growth or a company that has no profit as yet, while it develops its market or its product. A no-dividend policy does not of course necessarily mean a low or (no) share price, since the share will have value based on expectations as evidenced by Internet stocks.

Residual

As discussed earlier, residual would suit a company that has a fluctuating need for retained earnings but is happy to pay away any surplus that is not needed in any one year.

Constant

There are several variations on the constant theme. There could be a constant dividend with increments every so often when the management is confident that the new level may be maintained. There is the constant increase perhaps specified as a 5% growth per annum or even as a growth rate tied to the retail price index. Any shortfalls in profit in poor years being made up from retained earnings or borrowings. This presupposes a company with some balance sheet strength and reasonable access, when needed, to the debt markets.

Special dividends

There are occasions when management wishes to return value to shareholders but does not wish to raise an expectation that this will happen every year. This can be done by issuing a scrip or special dividend while making it clear that this is a one-off distribution for a particular reason. Another way could be by utilising share buy-backs. Obviously, for those shareholders that sell there has been a return of value. For those that do not choose to sell, or are not given the opportunity, the share price in the market should reflect an increased price due to the purchasing activities (but may not).

Conclusion

A reading of the comments in the financial press leaves no doubt that, whatever the theoretical arguments, dividend policy is regarded as important. With this in mind, it is also clear that the financial managers of a company should have a clearly defined dividend policy. This should be clearly communicated to the market and should be justified in the context of the industry that the company operates in, tempered by the particular circumstances of the company involved and its needs for investment and its cash generative abilities. Once defined and communicated, the management should then deliver.

References and further reading

Black F and Scholes M 1974 'The effects of dividend yield and dividend policy on common stock prices and returns', *Journal of Financial Economics*, **1** (May).

Brealey RA and Myers SC 1999 *Principles of Corporate Finance*, 6th edn, McGraw Hill, Maidenhead.

Elton E and Gruber M 1970 'Marginal stockholder tax rates and the clientele effect', *Review of Economic Statistics*, **52** (February).

Lintner J 1956 'Distribution of incomes of corporations among dividends, retained earnings and taxes', *American Economic Review*, no. 46 (May), 97–113.

Litzenberger R and Ramaswamy K 1982 'The effects of dividends on common stock prices. Tax effects or information effects, *Journal of Finance* **xxxvii** (2), May.

Marsh TA and Merton RC 1987 'Dividend behaviour for the aggregate stock market', *Journal of Business*, no. 60, January.

Miller MH and Modigliani F 1961 'Dividend policy, growth, and the valuation of shares, *Journal of Business* **xxxiv**, October.

Miller MH and Rock K 1965 'Dividend policy under asymmetric information, *Journal of Finance* **xi** (4), September.

Rosenberg B and Marathe V 1979 'Tests of capital asset pricing model hypotheses', in *Research in Finance* (edited by H Levy), JAI Press.

Ross SA 1977 'The determination of financial structure: the incentive-signalling approach', *Bell Journal of Economics*, **8**, 23–40.

Appendix 6.1

Share price	=	£3.30	
0.5% transaction cost	=	£0.0165	
Net receipt pre-tax	=	£3.2835	
£18000 needed	=	5627.7259 shares	
Check			
5627.7259 × £3.30	=	£18571.49547	
$^1/_2$ transaction cost	=	£9285.747	
Net pre-tax receipt			£18478.638
Original cost			
5627.7259 × £3.00	=	£16883.178	
Capital gain	=	£1595.46	
30% tax			£478.638
Net after-tax receipt			£18000.000

Appendix 6.2

A shareholder has two tax levels of

Income tax	40%
Capital gains tax	25%

A share in company A has, at the start of the year, a value of £1.00. During the year, 20p of earnings are added, which will be paid out as a dividend.

The net result for an income tax payer will be

Receive dividend	20p
Tax @ 40%	8p
Net receipt	12p

However, if the share is sold cum dividend, i.e. with the dividend going to the new holder of the share, the share will sell for £1.20.

The net result for a capital gains tax payer will be

Bought at	£1.00
Sold for	£1.20
Capital gain	20p
Capital gains tax	5p
Net receipt	15p

If both shareholders require a net 12p return, then in fact, at the start of the year, the capital gains tax payer would have been willing to pay £1.04.

Bought at	£1.04
Sold at	£1.20
Capital gain	16p
Capital gains tax	4p
Net receipt	12p

In other words, the share price, given a clientele of capital gains tax payers, will fall by 80% of the dividend, not by the full amount.

Chapter

7 Managing stakeholder perceptions

Introduction

This chapter is concerned with how a company can manage the perceptions of the stakeholders in the company and how an outside agency, which has the role of interpreting the company for outside shareholders, looks behind the figures to the reality. The Company Perspective is written by a manager with day-to-day responsibility for the financial management of the company and who is therefore concerned with how and to whom the message is communicated. In Rating Methodology – Moody's Tool Kit 'we see how the new hybrids are looked at by someone who acts on behalf of the investors in the company and is therefore concerned with accurately deciphering that message.

THE COMPANY PERSPECTIVE

The theory

One of the basic concepts in modern financial theory is that management – the company Board – acts in the interests of shareholders – the owners of the company – in order to maximise the current value of that company. A number of principles of investment, and of the financing of that investment, have been developed to facilitate the achievement of that objective, and they make up the major part of most modern texts on finance. They include: the use of current prices, especially 'present value'; the maximisation of net present values; the calculation of cost of capital, including risk and uncertainty in the equation (CAPM; see Chapter 1); the development of an optimal capital structure; and of a dividend policy, etc. These principles, it is claimed, can not only be used by the finance team and the Board only in arriving at major decisions, such as how much to borrow, what dividends to pay, and when to raise new equity, but also in setting the company's policies and practices in the area of short-term finance – borrowings, management of liquidity and hedging of interest and foreign exchange risks. These basic concepts and principles, then, provide the finance director, and treasurer with a tool-kit, which enables them to advise the Board on just how the company's resources should be spent, or invested, and on just how these resources should be obtained, i.e. the financing decision – in theory, at any rate.

The 'buts'

There is, however, another basic concept present in modern theory that tends to upset this somewhat happy picture. It is known as the agency problem and was referred to in Chapter 1 from an academic perspective, and, although it is often dismissed in a page or two in the texts, it calls for at least another mention here. While it does not go so far as to claim that sometimes management – the 'agents' – and shareholders are in open conflict, it does suggest that there often exists a gap in communications between them. It makes essentially the same point about relationships between management and the lenders to the company – banks and others.

If the agency problem is a real one, and most modern writers in corporate finance accept that it is, it tends to imply that markets are not quite as 'efficient' as modern theory requires them to be. Nevertheless, it is claimed that it evidences itself in discussions about compensation (options, performance bonuses, pension entitlements etc.), the pressure for ever greater disclosure, arguments over new equity issues and pre-emption rights, the dividend controversy, and as far as lenders are concerned, differences over interest charges and covenants. In the UK of late, the problem has been made more acute by the pressure being placed on management to take into account the claims of stakeholders other than shareholders, on an equal basis – the so-called 'inclusive approach'. It is by no means clear just how this new concept of management's role is supposed to work, but it is obvious that it is not going to resolve the agency problem, in the short term at any rate.

The real world

So much for the theoretical background – what is it like in the real world? In practice the treasurer will be following policies and guidelines he/she and the Board regard as sensible, effective and virtually ordained. They will include, for example, a reasonable dividend policy, fairly conservative gearing, i.e. the preservation of ample unused borrowing capacity, the appropriate mix of long-term and short-term debt, and of fixed-rate and floating-rate borrowings, some liquidity, and the ability to hedge foreign exchange and interest rate exposures etc. But in doing all that, utilising all the advice forthcoming from commercial and investment bankers, is there a danger that the financial manager will not be responding fully to the expectations of shareholders and other stakeholders in the company? That is the question we need to address, and it is easiest to take the shareholders and their expectations first.

Shareholders

This book is concerned mainly with the liabilities 'side' of the company balance sheet, in effect with the company's capital structure. The finance function is, of course, much involved in the assets side as well, i.e. in the investment of the company's resources. Treasurers will have, as one of their major roles, the management of the company's liquidity. It is also vital that the finance function takes the lead as far as the company's capital expenditures are concerned, in determining the company's cost of capital and in bringing home to management the special problems that arise in the financing of projects overseas. They will also be involved in deciding just how financing opportunities unique to specific projects ought to be dealt with. In addition, the finance team must play a major role in the 'buy or lease' decision, and also in deciding on divisional and project Betas to be used in the capital budgeting programme. In all of this, the basic principle that will be followed will be that the goal is to maximise net present values. This will be done using a cost of capital that embodies the return that shareholders expect for the degree of risk they have taken on and which they could realise by investing elsewhere. In short, shareholders' expectations will be realised if the basic principles are followed.

Turning to the liabilities side of the balance sheet, again the principal assumption behind modern financial theory is that management acts in the interests of the shareholders – but just what are those interests? Ever since capitalism moved ahead from the stage when most firms were fairly small, the owner or owners were easily identifiable and more often than not were active proprietors, to a situation where companies found themselves with numerous owners or shareholders, it has become increasingly difficult for management to be fully aware of the needs or interests of the owners.

In Britain, for example, the rise to pre-eminence, since the early 1960s, of the institutions – insurance companies, pension funds, unit trusts and investment trusts – as the effective owners of 'UK PLC', while it ought to have eased the problem, has not. Institutions, it is said, now own about 70% of the UK's corporate sector; many companies find themselves looking at share registers which show five to ten institutions holding around 40% of the equity. In a number of cases, a single institution will stand out above the rest with a holding of around 20%. But in spite of their becoming endowed with this possession of real power, the institutions have been curiously reluctant to make use of it. It is difficult, for example, even in the case of a specific company, to elicit the institutions' views on its strategy, investment policy, gearing, dividend policy, acquisition and/or divestment aspirations, and possible resort to shareholders for additional finance. To some, this is the direct outcome of modern fund managers' emphasis on short termism, and the absolute priority of liquidity. In effect, becoming too committed to a company's basic financial policies makes it difficult for a shareholder to walk away by selling, should the need arise. To an extent, also, it is the result of the necessity of not becoming an 'insider', again prompted by the liquidity consideration, and to some extent dictated by bodies such as the Stock Exchange. This is the real nub of the agency problem, the communications gap that exists between the effective owners and the management. It is even more difficult to arrive at a common list of interests for the numerous small shareholders, though in most cases the problem boils down to the question: 'Is their principal aim income or capital gains?'

In this situation management's aim must be, not to sit back and accept the status quo, but to do all that it can to foster good relations with the shareholder body via open and good communications. This is much more than just the production of a full and informative Annual Report, and of painstaking regard for the shareholders at the AGM. Obviously, it is the job of the chairman and the chief executive to impart to the world the company's basic business strategy, and the ways in which it intends to succeed, at public meetings, in announcements, and at more private meetings with institutions, the financial press and so on. But it falls on the finance director and his/her team to explain the company's financial strategies and policies, and to try to satisfy shareholders that their interests do coincide with those of management.

This role has become even more of a necessity in recent years as a result of the ever widening acceptance in financial and business circles of the tenets of 'shareholder value'. Those who have developed the various shareholder value concepts have created what is virtually a new school of finance and nowadays strategies are built up and businesses are evaluated using it, even compensation schemes for senior management are structured around it, and investor relations programmes are guided by it. It began as a critique of traditional methods of evaluation – ROCE, growth in EPS, Price: Earnings ratios etc; it claims to be solidly based on cash flows, and to possess the most logical methods of evaluating businesses, developing strategies, judging acquisitions, etc. It is vital that the chief executive and the finance director and his team are able to talk sensibly about the company's performance in relation to Economic Value Added (EVA), Economic Value to EBITDA and share Price to Free Cash Flow per Share, for example.

There are four main concerns, which the financial team needs to concentrate on when explaining financial strategy: equity strategy; debt strategy; short-term strategy; and organisation.

Equity strategy

Here the first priority is to explain, and be convincing about, the company's dividend policy. In spite of all the theoretical argument to the effect that dividends are irrelevant, they clearly matter a great deal to many shareholders, and even to sophisticated institutional fund managers. The company must have a convincing story on dividend policy – something to the effect that dividends will be increased in line with long-term growth in earnings, and certainly to beat inflation, is usual. In most cases, it is also necessary to give some indication of what sort of pay-out ratio the company regards as an appropriate target, over, of course, a long period. Linked with its dividend policy is the company's attitude towards the raising of additional equity finance. All too often, companies give the impression that they are confident of achieving a growth rate that is perfectly satisfactory as far as investors are concerned, solely from retentions and additional borrowings, only to have to fall back on a substantial rights issue. A more rational presentation of the role of retentions and debt, supplemented by additional new capital as appropriate to finance major moves such as an acquisition, will be more rewarding in the long run. In addition, the finance team needs to have thought through the company's dynamics. A retention rate and a level of profitability that, for example, indicate a growth rate well above that of the company's basic business need to be explained. Diversification is no longer popular – clearly situations like this lead into the need for openness about the company's basic strategy.

Debt strategy

The finance director will find it easier to be convincing about the company's gearing policy – its policy on its gearing ratio, interest cover target and what it sees as its sustainable debt capacity. It is difficult, however, to get, even from the institutions, a shareholder reaction on this question, and they are certainly not prepared to commit themselves on, for example, an optimal gearing level for the company. Probably one of the most rewarding points the finance director can make is to confirm that the company has a gearing policy, and that having departed from it in order to finance, say, a major acquisition, it has in place plans to achieve a reasonably quick return to the normal level of borrowing.

Short-term strategy

In the corporate governance debate, it is becoming increasingly important to satisfy shareholders that the company's short-term financing strategy, systems and controls are adequate. This is partly due to heavy losses suffered by some major companies in their financial hedging operations, and partly because of the emphasis on financial risk, and the consequent need for adequate controls. The topics that have to be covered are liquidity objectives and management, policies on interest rate risk and foreign currency exposure, the short- and medium-term facilities available, and the major covenants the company has accepted (and why they ought not to prove too restrictive).

Organisation

For obvious reasons, shareholders are likely to be even more interested in the way in which finance is managed in the company. For example, what delegation of powers exists? What controls are in place? What reports are made, especially to the Board and the audit committee? How are major risk areas identified, and what policies are in place for coping with these risks?

Much of this, fortunately, tends to coincide with the greater degree of disclosure required from companies in their annual reports, in, for example, the Operating and Financial Review, and in the Board's statement on Internal Controls. But institutional shareholders, in particular, are requiring clear and convincing explanations of the company's policies and practices in addition to what is said in the Annual Report.

In all of this, the basic underlying imperative must be to convince shareholders and investors that the financial priority is the achievement of cash flow returns in excess of 'hurdle rates' so as to create a premium for the owners. This, in turn, entails the realisation of a satisfactory long-term growth rate, and it is important to repeat what may seem to a finance man an obvious message, namely, that a shareholder's return on his/her investment consists of the dividend yield plus growth. This is probably the most difficult area for the company in its relationship with shareholders, because it needs to be convincing in answering a number of questions such as: what rate of growth should flow from retentions? What is likely to be the role of acquisitions? How are acquisitions likely to be financed? And, in what circumstances would the company resort to shareholders for that finance? In addition, if the company's recent track record indicates that, in order to achieve a satisfactory growth rate of earnings, dividends and, hopefully, of share value in the future, it needs to 'turn around' significantly, it must also give an indication of just how it plans to do that.

Analysts

It is convenient to consider how the company needs to manage its relationship with analysts, along with the shareholders. There can be no doubt that analysts are a vital cog in the whole machinery of the 'efficient markets' of today. The essence of that efficiency is the speed at which new information about a company is reflected in its share price. It follows that good relations with them are important. Even more crucial, however, is the point that all should be treated equally. Some tend to concentrate on past trends in rates of return, retention rates and so on and, in order to test whether they are likely to continue or not, will be probing for information on up-to-date trends in sales, profit margins, etc. Others tend to focus on P/E ratios and projections of EPS in order to arrive at a justifiable price. Yet others are becoming increasingly interested in cash flows and projections of them, probing for estimates of capital expenditure, etc. in order to attempt some sort of DCF approach to the company's valuation. The treasurer may not always be the investor relations manager for the company, but clearly these matters cannot be properly managed without his/her involvement. It is, of course, important that no forecasts are given, and indeed that detailed information that is not already in the public domain is not made available. The real role of the finance team is to provide guidance to the analysts.

Bankers and lenders

There is one possible attitude towards bankers and lenders, which is understandable and which might also seem to be justifiable, namely that they and their perceptions do not call for special consideration. This is because, unlike other stakeholders in the company, before lending to the company they impose detailed, often strangling, covenants and, in many cases, insist on security or some other collateral, and thus in a sense look after themselves. There is also the fact that, since the invention of 'floating interest rates', a good deal of the risk implicit in lending has been removed, because much of medium- and long-term lending has, at least as far as the interest element in the return is concerned, become short term. According to 'agency theory', lenders insist on their covenants, and on their 'prior' or 'floating' charges, because they are afraid that should a financial emergency arise, owners and management might work together against the interests of the company's creditors. The example that is normally quoted is a decision to take on a very risky investment rather than a safe one, because, in the event of failure, the loss will fall on creditors, while success will mean gain, mainly for the owners. If this is correct, it is worrying. In the early days of the development of the theory of corporate finance, much emphasis was placed on the need for understanding by corporate financiers of the concerns of lenders, and of the necessity of good relationships with them if restructuring, break-up and eventual liquidations were to be avoided. The failures of the 1960s and again of the 1980s were in many cases the result of companies' ignoring this basic lesson.

It is also a basic principle of corporate finance that the company must have access to additional funds even in the worst of times – hence its committed facilities. It must also be able to prove to its lenders that it will be able to keep its total borrowing within a sustainable level, i.e. the level it can service, in the depth of a recession. Moreover, if the company's business is capital intensive or cyclical, it will have to be able to justify a degree of long-term debt in its capital structure. The result is that the treasurer must manage the perceptions of bankers and lenders, in the interests of the company, in the following areas: amount of finance; covenants; long-term relationships and costs.

Amount of finance

Here, the company will almost certainly want to emphasise the fact that its policy is conservative. Conservative in the sense that committed facilities are there to cope with emergencies on top of its base borrowings, and that future expectations and cash flows have been significantly discounted because uncertainty is a keynote of business.

Covenants

It is interesting that while bankers tend to concentrate on a company's cash-generating capacity when deciding whether to lend or not, and how much to lend, they also tend to fall back on accounting figures and ratios when detailing the covenants they need. Their prime concern is, of course, the preservation of the company's capital base, because if the equity or shareholders' funds are intact, so will their loan or investment be. In this connection, then, the need is to convince the lender of the soundness of the company's accounting policies, as well as of the soundness of its financial strength and financial policies.

Long-term relationships

The cost to the company of establishing the right understanding with bankers and other lenders will not be worthwhile if the relationship is a short-term one only. The company will need committed banks, just as the banks in turn need committed customers. The effort required to establish the appropriate number and pattern of major relationship, or 'house', banks can be considerable, and maintaining those relationships calls for constant attention. In exchange for a prime position in the company's short-term investing, borrowing and hedging activities, those banks should be committed to assisting with acquisitions and not assisting predators.

Costs

It may seem strange to place 'costs' last in this list of lenders' perceptions. They are there because, to the extent that these might be a special situation for the company as regards the cost of finance, it will depend on the factors already mentioned, for example maintaining the relationship over time. Cost must, of course, always be a function of the market, and of the company's financial strength, track records and prospects. But, if relationship banks feel that the company has delivered in the past, not only in the business it has provided, but also with forecasts of requirements and in its attention to covenants etc., it should be productive in terms of keeping overall costs to a minimum.

Sources of finance

If the emphasis in this analysis seems to be on the creation, development and maintenance of what might be termed traditional sources of finance, it is because the principal job of the finance function must be to maintain the continuity of a flow of cash. This is so that the company is able to maintain its strategy even during downturns in business. In an emergency, it is either too late or too time consuming, to establish new sources of finance. Speedy access to funds from traditional sources is what is called for. It follows that the major problems the finance team will have to address are likely to be banks and medium-term finance.

Banks

How many and which? Any medium-term facility is likely to involve too many for them all to become 'house banks' and the company will have to establish, and manage, 'primary' and 'secondary' lists.

Medium-term finance

After building up an armoury of medium-term facilities, the company will want more permanent and probably fixed-rate finance. The obvious solution, especially for the medium-sized company, is a private placement. These are difficult, if not impossible to arrange in the UK, with the result that the company must decide whether, for example, to turn to the US market, and then use the swap market if it does not want a dollar liability. A move beyond even that position, to a bond issue of some description, involves not only taking on more risks, but also having to cope with a different set of lenders' perceptions.

Rating agencies

It is at this point that a 'rating' can become crucial. If the company is going to regard the bond market as one of those sources of finance it would like to have access to even in difficult times, a rating will be essential. In fact, a rating can be regarded as an asset, and the view that obtaining one involves detailed questions is really beside the point. It is interesting to note that there are times (for example, because of the necessity for commercial banks to be constantly trying to match their open positions in derivatives) that companies with BBB ratings can insist on being taken seriously. In addition, the rating process can often bring home to the company some deficiencies in its own systems. Credibility with a rating agency is established more by achieving realistic, if somewhat conservative, forecasts, than by submitting bullish projections and then failing to match them. A rating will be compulsory if the company intends to move into the US markets and establish a presence there on a continuing basis, but it is also becoming increasingly significant in the 'international market'.

Other stakeholders

It was always implicit in the prime objective of the management of a company – the maximisation of the shareholders' interests – that concern for the needs of employees (including pensioners), customers, suppliers and others, was necessary, and would impact favourably on the shareholders' interests. But of late, the so-called 'stakeholder concept' has been afforded much more emphasis. The concept that concern for stakeholders other than the shareholder must be in the long-term interest of the company, and as a result be of benefit to the shareholder as well, has been modified. There has been much analysis of the different systems of corporate governance that have emerged in, for example, Germany and Japan. Following from this, a view has gained ground to the effect that the company should be managed so as to take equal notice of the interests of all stakeholders and for the equal benefit of all of them. In the UK, this so-called 'inclusive approach' has attracted a good deal of attention, and at times seems to have been supported by the Labour Party, as well as by some leading companies. It is by no means clear precisely how it is supposed to work, nor what legal changes will be called for if it is to be implemented fully. Nor is it obvious just how many 'stakeholders' a company's management must include in its considerations – nor how they will be represented, if at all. Nevertheless, even at this stage in this new development, the perceptions of 'stakeholders' are having an increasing influence on management, as follows.

Employees

It is generally recognised as an attribute of a good and responsible company that it should not only try to meet the aspirations of its employees, but also consult with them as far as is possible. Consultation does not of course, necessarily imply trade union involvement. The finance team's involvement in this activity can be considerable, not only in bringing home to employees the realities of the company's financial position and the possibilities in the future, the need for dividends, the scope for further borrowing, etc., but also in convincing employees of the importance of future developments. This could include both the need for overseas expansion and for the restructuring of the business from time to time. The increasing involvement of employees in various incentive schemes – profit sharing, savings-related options and all employee option schemes, for example – has led to a closer identification of the interests of employees in understanding the financial dynamics of the company so that they are in a position to accept the main objectives of the management. The fact that a number of UK companies have already moved to establish 'Works Councils' on European lines is indicative.

Pensioners, as a stakeholder group, can be conveniently grouped with employees. It is probably true to say that only a financial person – and a patient one at that – can hope to explain the position of the pension fund of a company to existing pensioners, and to potential ones – the employees. The necessary funding, principally by the company, in order to secure the promised scale and level of benefits, the assumptions made by actuaries in arriving at that funding and the possible ways of coping with a surplus, if there is one, are such complex matters that the finance team must be involved if serious misunderstandings are not to arise. The same holds true of explanations of the investment policies and the hoped for results pursued by the fund's investment managers, and these days, of the rewards to top management in pension fund benefits.

Suppliers

Most of the requirements of suppliers, as a stakeholder group, will have to be met by the manufacturing and commercial functions within the company. But payment terms, the credit permitted to the company, will not only be vetted by the finance function, the actual implementation of those terms will have to be policed by that function. It will be up to the finance team to help ensure that, via an efficient system for ensuring prompt payment by the company, a loyal team of suppliers is maintained.

Customers

Here also, it will be the role of the finance function to make certain that credit given to customers is appropriate, that payment terms are met, that doubtful and bad debts are monitored, and that a proper system of credit evaluation is in place. If these systems are fair, and are managed efficiently without becoming aggressive, customers should feel that their interests are taken into account as well as the company's.

Others

These include local authorities, local communities and groups of various kinds and, indeed, the community at large. Many decisions by the company affecting such stakeholders will be largely financially motivated, e.g. location and relocation decisions, redundancies with a particular local impact, sales of businesses or plants, closures, environmental initiatives and so on. In these, the finance team will be called upon to explain part, at least, of the company's decision, and to make it clear that long-term survival is the objective. The particular problems that arise when the company is planning expansion overseas, while standing still or contracting at home, have already been mentioned.

Conclusion

Much of what has been said on the management of stakeholder perception in relation to the company's balance sheet must seem to boil down to common sense. Indeed, much of the actual practice of finance in companies, when compared with the complex theory often found in textbooks, does boil down to just that. But as far as the finance team is concerned, when developing the company's capital structure and in trying to marry stakeholder aspirations with what is seen as the company's objectives, the major problem areas are probably:

- Dividend policy: balancing the requirements of the shareholders with those of the lenders, and of management.
- Finance strategy and policies: the extent to which these can be revealed to shareholders (especially the institutions) and to employees, because of concerns over confidentiality, and the 'insider' problem.
- Covenants: matching the deemed needs of the lenders with the business imperatives of flexibility and manoeuvrability.
- Banking relationships: the maintenance of the right core group of 'relationship' or 'house' banks for the company.
- Take-over threat: essentially a matter of relationships with the institutions. Bearing in mind their tendency, in the end, to accept a 'good' offer, the finance team needs to have in place not only a 'defence' plan, but also a continuing programme aimed at convincing them that the company's long-term plans are right, and are capable of sensible financing.

The final thought in this whole area must be that massive generalisations are not possible and, if attempted, might well prove misleading. Every company is different and must, to an extent, cope with its own particular stakeholders in its own way.

RATING METHODOLOGY – MOODY'S TOOL KIT: A FRAMEWORK FOR ASSESSING HYBRID SECURITIES

There are many different stakeholders in a company, and it is not the purpose of this book to tease out all the nuances of corporate governance in this area. However, the rating agencies have been mentioned a number of times and, since they are acting on behalf of some of the stakeholder groups, it is worth seeing how they think about at least one aspect of the capital structure discussion, that is the treatment of debt that has equity features. Many issues are brought out in the following discussion but what is especially interesting is the way in which those responsible for analysing company balance sheets are more and more looking behind the accounting figures. They do this to work out what the real impact of various instruments is on the debt service capability of an organisation and, hence, what is the real position of the debt holder and the equity holder.

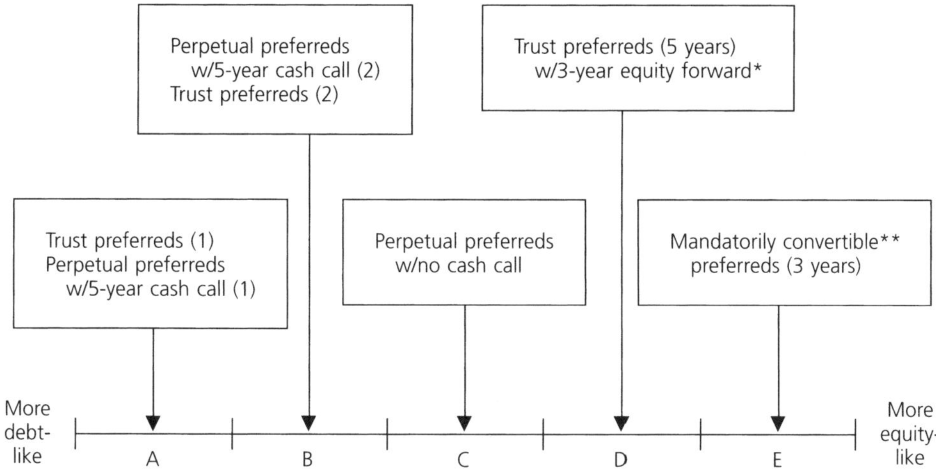

(1) For financial institutions and high-grade corporates.
(2) For high yield and lower-rated investment grade issuers.
* Fixed number of shares issued. Assumes that equity remains a permanent part of the capital structure.
** Assumes that equity remains a permanent part of the capital structure.

7.1 Moody's debt–equity continuum (Instruments within baskets are not in rank order)

Overview

Hybrid securities, which combine the features of both debt and equity, can take numerous forms including preferred securities, convertible subordinated debt, or preferred instruments that mandatorily convert to equity. Hybrids continue to grow in importance as financing vehicles as issuers seek lower cost alternatives to equity capital. The popularity of hybrids is evidenced by their rapid growth; through October 1999, $49.6 billion were issued compared to $30.9 billion in 1995.[1]

When a new hybrid security is introduced to the market, Moody's is asked to assess the impact of the instrument on an issuer's capital structure. The questions frequently centre on the amount of 'equity credit' that the instrument provides based on its equity-like characteristics. In response to these questions, our analytical framework or Tool Kit for assessing hybrid securities is described. The application of the Tool Kit provides greater insight into how Moody's views several well-known instruments and also provides a benchmark for assessing new hybrid securities as they are developed.

Because hybrid securities are generally not pure debt or pure equity, Moody's uses the Tool Kit to place a particular security on the debt–equity continuum (see Fig. 7.1), which is used to calibrate the traditionally 'grey

1 Primarily includes preferreds, trust preferreds, and convertible securities as reported by Securities Data Company.

area' between the two extremes of debt and equity. To accomplish this task, the instrument is first broken down into its basic features including maturity, call option, conversion features, deferral features, and its priority of claim in bankruptcy. These basic attributes are then compared to the characteristics of pure equity – no maturity, no ongoing payments that could trigger a default if unpaid, and loss absorption for all other creditors – to see how closely equity is replicated.

After the instrument's features are identified, it is necessary to consider how they are combined. Moody's determines the relative weight of each of the instrument's characteristics and then places the instrument in one of five baskets ranging from A to E on the debt–equity continuum. By stripping out all issuer-specific considerations, the continuum provides a broad, generic ranking for hybrid securities on a relative basis and a determination of their potential impact on the capital structure at issuance. However, the relative ranking of hybrid securities provided by their placement on the debt–equity continuum is only a starting point in the determination of ratings. Once the characteristics of the hybrid security are assessed, the instrument is viewed within the context of each issuer's overall credit fundamentals. In many instances, the instruments in and of themselves do not make a difference in the rating outcome.

Moody's always considers a company's capital structure in assessing its credit fundamentals, but capital is by no means the sole consideration and, in fact, it is probably not the most important factor. In the determination of ratings, other factors are assessed, including the issuer's market position, its competitive advantages and disadvantages, revenue growth potential, cost structure, relative sensitivity to the business cycle, and the quality of management. **The ability of a company to generate sufficient cash flow on an ongoing basis to cover its financial obligations is a key determinant.** How a company positions itself to generate earnings and cash flow – the steps that it takes to secure its future, including business investments, capital spending, and acquisitions, and how these investments are financed – form the basis for a rating opinion.

In determining ratings:

- Capital is only one factor.
- Cash flow generating capability is key.
- The focus is on the hybrid's impact on cash flow.

Consequently, Moody's focuses on the effect that a hybrid security will have on a company's cash flow when it evaluates the potential benefits that the company may obtain from using the hybrid. The analyst also considers the underlying rationale for issuing the security, taking into account factors such as the anticipated use of proceeds and the relative importance of the hybrid within the capital structure.

Introduction

The purpose of this Rating Methodology is twofold. The first is to describe the basics of the Tool Kit and how Moody's uses it to place hybrid securities on the debt–equity continuum. This provides greater insight into how several well-known instruments are viewed and also provides a benchmark for assessing new hybrid securities as they are developed. The second is to discuss the relative importance of the capital structure in the determination of ratings.

Section 1 covers the nature of equity and how hybrid securities seek to replicate equity through their various characteristics. Section 2 provides a discussion of the thought process Moody's uses to determine where a hybrid security is placed on the debt–equity continuum once its characteristics are identified. Section 3 applies the Tool Kit to two well-known hybrid securities, trust preferred securities and mandatorily convertible preferred securities. Section 4 discusses the potential impact of hybrid securities on an issuer's ratings, Section 5 includes a case study, and Section 6 summarizes the main points in the report.

Section 1: The nature of equity and its replication in hybrids

A The nature of equity

To understand the concept of 'equity credit', it is necessary to take common stock, the purest form of equity, and define its core characteristics. By isolating equity's characteristics and understanding why they are beneficial to an issuer's financial flexibility, we can consider how successfully hybrids replicate equity. From a credit perspective, the three principal characteristics of equity are: no ongoing payments, no maturity (no principal repayment) and significant loss absorption.

No ongoing payments

An issuer can reduce or eliminate dividend payments on common stock. The ability to cut or eliminate fixed interim payments is a characteristic of common stock that can provide significant financial flexibility to an issuer. Companies typically go to great lengths to pay, and to increase steadily, their dividends on common stock. Nevertheless, in a crisis situation, the issuer can elect to skip its dividend without triggering an event of default. In a start-up situation, an equity-funded company can skip dividend payments until it is generating profits. This is not the case with traditional debt. If a company cannot make its required interest payments on a particular debt instrument, this is usually grounds for default on that instrument and for cross-default to other debt instruments.

No maturity (no principal repayment)
Common stock does not have to be repaid. Unlike debt, which usually has a fixed term, common stock does not give the investor a fixed claim on a firm's cash flow, either for a gradual amortisation or for repayment in full. The gradual amortisation of an obligation places an ongoing fixed demand on the cash flow of a borrower. This obligation introduces the risk of default, cross default to other debt, and even bankruptcy. The repayment in full of a debt obligation can be a major credit event for a borrower, placing a severe demand on cash flow. Common stock imposes no such demands.

Significant loss absorption
Common stock provides the highest loss absorption characteristics of any class of security because its holders are the last to receive distributions in a liquidation. In addition, common equity may provide a cushion sufficient to reduce the likelihood of a liquidation event. The equity of an issuer is comprised of common stock or owners' interests and its value depends on the ongoing ability of the issuer to generate future earnings and cash flow. Equity is also the residual value of an issuer after deducting all liabilities. It provides a cushion to support ongoing business activities and to absorb the shocks of any unforeseen events. In a distressed situation, equity provides the first layer of loss absorption.

While hybrids seek to replicate the above three characteristics, equity has a fundamentally different value dynamic than debt. Equity represents ownership of the business, and therefore, offers theoretically unlimited appreciation as well as depreciation, instead of the fixed value that debt offers (assuming that the investor holds the debt to maturity). Furthermore, equity provides the capacity for internal capital growth through profit retention to finance business operations, which reduces a company's need to issue new equity or debt.

B The replication of equity in hybrids

Traditional preferred stock
Perhaps the earliest developed, and long the most prevalent, form of hybrid security is preferred stock. In its traditional form, preferred stock is issued directly by the parent or operating company. It is characterised by a **deeply subordinated legal claim**, which provides some loss absorption, and a **fixed after-tax dividend that may be deferred** at the issuer's option (subject to simultaneous suspension of the common dividend) without causing a legal default. Preferred stock holders usually **do not have voting rights** unless dividends have been skipped. In terms of maturity, preferred stocks can be either **long-dated or perpetual**, typically also including an issuer call option. In addition, some preferred stock may be **convertible**

to common stock at the investor's option or on a mandatory basis at maturity.

As is evident from the above, preferred stock, with its various permutations, has been designed to provide the issuer with a package of more or less 'equity-like' features. These features may result in greater financial flexibility for the issuer in comparison to straight debt. In practice, however, investors expect most preferred stock to perform as quasi-fixed income securities with relatively stable valuations and minimal expected credit loss. Accordingly, issuance has been concentrated among high-grade issuers, including many regulated utilities and financial institutions. In response to investor demand, Moody's has provided credit ratings on preferred stock for many years, reinforcing the perception that such securities are expected to perform in a fixed income-like manner.

Economic substance versus accounting treatment

Preferred stock is a good example of the inconsistency that sometimes exists between the accounting treatment of a security and its true economic substance. Standard accounting conventions in the US and most other jurisdictions treat such securities on the balance sheet as equity rather than liabilities. However, from a credit analysis perspective, the accountants' balance sheet classification is not as important as the way the security is expected to perform in terms of future cash flows, and, as a secondary matter for certain high-yield issuers, the loss absorption, which may be expected in the event of a business failure. This focus on economic substance has always been key to Moody's analysis of preferred stock, particularly as it relates to the ratings evaluation of senior classes of debt. Clearly, there are various forms of preferred stock, and Moody's strives to recognize and assess the differing economic characteristics of each accurately, irrespective of accounting classifications.

Today's hybrids often based on preferred stock model

An understanding of preferred stock is especially relevant in today's expanding world of hybrids because many currently popular structures are based on the preferred stock model, usually with additional engineering to create a tax deduction for the ongoing dividend or coupon. Moreover, the way that Moody's analyzes these hybrids is similar to the way that preferred stock is analyzed – by focusing on the economic substance. We recognize that hybrids can provide economic benefits to issuers. Because the fixed payments are generally tax-deductible, hybrid securities can lower an issuer's cost of capital (compared to traditional preferred securities and common equity) and enhance its after-tax cash flow. However, these benefits do not necessarily mean that the hybrids constitute 'equity'.

The sections that follow provide an overview of some of the features found in many of today's popular hybrid structures and the way in which they, individually and as a package, provide a combination of flexibility to the issuer and value to the investor.

Interest or dividend deferral

A deferral clause gives an issuer the option to defer the payment of interest or preferred dividend, which is otherwise due on an agreed payment date. This option is often conditioned on the simultaneous suspension of the issuer's common stock dividends. Unlike a missed interest payment on debt, the deferral does not constitute a legal default and may continue for a limited period of time (typically, five years for trust preferred securities issued in the US) or indefinitely (as with traditional preferred stock). The deferred payments may be cumulative or non-cumulative.

The contractual ability to defer interest or dividend payments on hybrid securities is often viewed as a positive feature at a time of financial distress. However, at the time the instrument is issued, the instrument may not make the same contribution to financial flexibility as does the ability to defer or eliminate dividends on common stock.

History shows that the deferral option is not likely to be used and therefore, tends to provide limited, if any, meaningful benefit to banks, other financial institutions and high-grade corporate issuers. Most high-grade companies make a distinction between preferred and common dividends and will go to great lengths during times of stress to make interest payments on their junior debt and dividend payments on preferred securities. This is particularly true in confidence-sensitive industries such as banking and financial services, which generally have a continuous need to access the short-term funding markets. For such issuers, the exercise of an interest deferral feature could have a dramatically negative impact on investors' confidence, and limit or destroy the institution's ability to access critical funding sources.

Still, the ability to defer interest or preferred dividends can be a valuable benefit to lower investment-grade and high-yield borrowers. For such issuers, cash flow generation tends to be weaker and the likelihood of an economic need to suspend payments tends to be greater. In addition, the potential for reputational damage that might spark a funding crisis for a high-grade company is a less prominent concern for most lower-rated issuers.

The deferral of interest or dividend payments can be either cumulative (payable in cash or 'in kind' securities) or non-cumulative. Under a cumulative deferral structure, missed interest or dividend payments remain a liability of the issuer and typically accrue interest. In addition, the issuer will be unable to make payments on other, more junior, forms of capital without first paying the deferred and accrued interest or dividends. In the case of non-cumulative deferral, the deferred payments do not remain a liability of the issuer and are permanently forgone.

A non-cumulative deferral structure replicates common stock more closely than a cumulative deferral structure because unpaid common dividends do not accrue. From the perspective of an issuer, the non-cumulative deferral feature offers greater financial flexibility because future cash flows need not be diverted to fund old, accrued liabilities.

Zero coupon structures

Zero coupon bonds do not provide an option to the issuer regarding the timing of payment. Under a zero coupon structure, the issuer does not make ongoing interest payments in cash. Rather, the interest payments accrue as a liability of the issuer at a pre-determined rate, and both principal and accrued interest are due in full at maturity or earlier redemption.

These structures are often employed to finance a project that will not come on stream, and therefore will not generate cash, for several years. They also may be used by high-yield issuers that need some short-term cash flow relief. While the lack of ongoing cash payment requirements may improve cash flow coverage in the short term, the large future cash payment at maturity may offset the positive effects of the interest payment deferral.

Perpetual maturity

One way to attempt to replicate the 'no maturity' feature of common stock is to create a hybrid security that is perpetual or permanent in nature. This feature provides financial flexibility to an issuer by eliminating a major credit event – the need to repay or refinance the principal amount. Therefore, Moody's considers a perpetual maturity to be a positive feature in terms of replicating equity. Of course, there is still an ongoing interest obligation, which must be serviced indefinitely, and the possible need to satisfy a creditor's claim immediately in the event of a default, cross-default, change in ownership or other form of reorganization of the issuer.

In addition, perpetual securities often incorporate an issuer call option, which may result in replacement with a term security (albeit at a lower cost) or even outright cash repayment. While either of these call events is likely to occur only when the issuer's financial condition remains sound, they could represent significant changes from the perspective of a shorter-term creditor. Furthermore, the perpetual term is even less valuable when the security incorporates an interest 'step-up' clause, which increases the likelihood of a call.

Long-dated maturity

A question that is frequently asked is, 'When does maturity become immaterial?' or 'When is there no material difference between a long-dated security and a perpetual security?' The answer is that a security with an extremely long maturity and no ongoing amortisation requirements may offer the same quality of capital as a perpetual security. The definition of 'extremely long' depends on the maturity of the issuer's other debt, on its likely ability to refinance, on industry practices, and on company-specific factors such as the issuer's position on the ratings spectrum.

Investor put feature

Put features provide considerable value to the investor at the expense of the issuer's flexibility. As a result, they detract from the equity-like characteristics that the security may otherwise feature. A put allows an investor to demand repayment of an obligation in full before the stated maturity. If an investor exercises the put, the issuer faces a potentially major claim on cash flow, similar to the payment in full of an obligation due at maturity. This may raise the possibility of a default or the need to refinance with another form of debt, most likely at a higher cost, which increases cash flow requirements.

Mandatory conversion to common shares

By their terms, mandatory convertible securities automatically convert to a fixed number of the issuer's common shares on the maturity date, which is typically a relatively short three to five years. Such a conversion feature is highly equity-like, as there is no potential refinancing requirement or repayment from the issuer's cash flow. In addition, the fixed exchange ratio and the short term to maturity indicate management's intention to raise incremental common equity, usually with a known level of earnings dilution.

The equity benefit of the mandatory conversion feature increases progressively as maturity approaches. By that time, it may become clear whether or not the equity will remain a permanent part of the capital structure rather than be offset by other changes to the capital structure such as share repurchases and the issuance of debt.

Some recent hybrids have incorporated mandatory conversion features through which the number of shares of common stock into which the hybrid converts is not fixed upfront. Rather, the number is adjusted based on the common stock market price at the conversion date so that the investor's principal investment is not at risk. These conversion features are generally viewed as less equity-like than the conversion to a fixed number of shares because the future performance of the stock price is unpredictable and it is difficult to evaluate management's resolve to tolerate an unknown level of future earnings dilution. The concern is lessened if the financing in question represents a very small proportion of the issuer's current market capitalisation. Nevertheless, a precipitous decline in a company's stock price could materially increase the dilutive impact of this kind of convertible security.

Optional conversion to common shares

Convertible debt and preferred stock offer the possibility of an exchange into common shares in the future, thus eliminating the need to repay the obligation with cash or to refinance it. Most of these securities are convertible at the investor's option, typically with a fixed conversion ratio and strike price at a moderate premium to the current market price for the issuer's common shares. These securities are attractive to issuers because investors will accept a lower coupon (compared to straight debt) in exchange for the option to convert their securities into common stock. In some instances, the reduction in the coupon can be substantial and result in meaningful after-tax cash flow savings.

When a company issues such convertible securities, management is signalling its intent to issue equity in the future. However, we accord less equity benefit to these convertibles than to mandatorily convertible securities because of the uncertainties involved. The timing of conversion or whether the bond will convert at all, depends on the issuer's operating performance and on stock market conditions, which determine whether or not the strike price will be achieved. In addition, even if the strike price is achieved, the conversion may not occur much prior to maturity, unless management has the ability to force the event by exercising a call option.

As a result, it is difficult to view this type of conversion feature as having much equity benefit **at the time of issuance**. If the convertible security subsequently becomes well 'in-the-money', i.e. the conversion price is below the current market price of the share, and management has the ability and willingness to force the conversion, its equity replication increases considerably. However, the history of convertibles shows that not all instruments that move into the money are ultimately converted into incremental new common equity, either because of a subsequent rapid drop in the share price or a change in plans by management, who may take steps to offset the new equity. Consequently, even when 'in-the-money', these types of convertible securities are not the same as extant common equity.

Junior priority of claim

Hybrid securities tend to have either a preferred or junior subordinated legal claim and therefore, rank below other classes of debt in the event of a bankruptcy reorganisation or liquidation. In other words, these securities typically will be the first to absorb loss in such scenarios, which can be a positive feature for lower-rated issuers. Senior lenders, such as banks, may be more willing to extend credit to speculative-grade issuers if subordinated securityholders are providing a layer of loss absorption. As a result, deeply subordinated securities may, in some instances, improve or maintain such an issuer's credit access.

The ability of a preferred security to absorb loss is evidenced by an estimate of its recovery rate in bankruptcy. For example, Moody's estimates that holders of preferred securities have recovered 10% of the par amount compared to 51% for senior unsecured bond holders and 33% for subordinated debt holders.

However, the issuance of 'pure' preferred securities has become relatively rare because the dividends on preferred securities are not tax-deductible. This results in a relatively expensive form of capital. Consequently, many hybrid securities combine a trust-issued preferred security with an underlying debt obligation of the parent or main operating company to generate a tax deduction. Trust preferred securities are typically viewed as debt claims of the parent company due to the loan between the trust and the parent company.

As a summary of the foregoing discussion, the chart below shows a sampling of individual features that appear in some hybrid securities, which are likely to be considered equity-like by Moody's.

Equity-like features seen in some hybrid securities

No maturity	No ongoing payments	Loss absorption
• Perpetual (non-callable) • Mandatory conversion (fixed conversion ratio)	• 5-yr interest/dividend deferral (non-cum)	• Preferred legal claim (direct, as opposed to trust-issued)

Section 2: Placing the hybrid security on the debt–equity continuum

As discussed in the previous section, many of the features typically incorporated in hybrid securities are unable to replicate fully the core characteristics of equity embedded in common stock. However, Moody's recognises that some hybrid features do provide equity-like benefits, and others provide a promise of further equity benefits in the near term. In addition, we recognise that sometimes the same feature may have more or less success at equity replication depending on the way it is combined with the other features of the security and/or the particular issuer's position on the credit spectrum.

For example, the behaviours of high-grade or high-yield issuers with respect to the hybrid may vary, and investor expectations could also differ. Moreover, there is an inherent expectation that highly rated issuers will honour all financial obligations, which reduces the flexibility that a particular hybrid may offer.

One way that Moody's summarises the benefits provided by a particular hybrid's features is through the relative position of the instrument on the debt–equity continuum.[2] Previous special comments have described the continuum, which is useful for ranking various hybrid securities as relatively more debt-like or relatively more equity-like in a generic or non-issuer specific sense. However, as stressed earlier, the specific impact any particular security may have on an issuer's capital structure and rating is judged on a case-by-case basis, and it depends on the individual circumstances surrounding each issuer. Specifically, the impact can be very different for a high-grade issuer than for a high-yield issuer.

We break down the debt–equity continuum into five broad baskets, with Basket A being the most debt-like and basket E being the most equity-like. For example, a hybrid security placed in Basket B is deemed to have a combination of features providing greater overall equity replication than a security placed in Basket A.

How does Moody's place a particular hybrid security on the continuum? The basic structure of our process is to understand the instrument including its specific features, how the features are combined, and the issuer's purpose for adding the hybrid to its capital structure. Central to this analysis is a comparison of the security's characteristics to the three core characteristics of equity ('no maturity', 'no ongoing payments', and 'loss absorption') to determine how well the hybrid's features replicate these equity characteristics. The ultimate goal is to understand how the security's features are expected to work together, particularly in a scenario of potential financial stress, to provide flexibility to the issuer and value to the investor.

The hybrid's characteristics *vis-à-vis* the 'no maturity', 'no ongoing payments', and 'loss absorption' characteristics of equity are ranked as either strong, moderate, weak, or none. For example, a mandatory convertible preferred security will receive a 'strong' ranking for 'no ongoing payments', reflecting both the ability to defer dividends prior to conversion and the end of preferred dividends after the conversion to common stock. In addition, the mandatory conversion of the preferred security to a fixed number of common shares produces a 'strong' ranking for the 'no maturity' characteristic as well. In contrast, a ranking of 'none' would mean there is no additional flexibility relative to straight senior debt.

Finally, the rankings for each of the three characteristics are combined with judgements regarding the use of proceeds and overall flexibility of the hybrid security to arrive at an overall equity replication score for the

2 The debt–equity continuum is first described in Moody's publication entitled 'Hybrid Securities: Debt or Equity?' dated August 1995.

security from A to E. We also compare the instrument to other instruments in the same basket to ensure consistency. These comparisons involve judgement rather than adherence to formulas.

For example, a hybrid that is deemed to have a strong degree of equity replication for each of the three equity characteristics is typically placed in either Basket D or E. But, a hybrid security that is strong in one dimension (for example, 'no maturity') and moderate or weak in the other two may also be placed in Basket D. In analysing the instruments, there is no common formula that applies more or less weight to a particular characteristic.

Section 3: Application of Moody's Tool Kit

To illustrate Moody's analytical process, it is useful to look at two specific examples, trust preferred securities, and mandatory convertible preferred stock.

Trust preferred securities (non-convertible)

Trust preferred securities frequently seen in the US market are designed to combine the tax deductibility of interest payments with financial flexibility similar to that of traditional preferred stock. Under a trust preferred structure, preferred securities are issued by a trust,[3] which lends proceeds to the parent company through a subordinated loan that is junior to all other debt of the parent. The terms of the preferred securities match the terms of the underlying subordinated loan. The parent makes tax-deductible interest payments sufficient to cover dividend payments, and also guarantees, on a subordinated basis, the payment of principal and dividends to the extent that there are funds in the trust. The other key features of these securities are:

- long maturity (for example, a 40-year bullet);
- typically callable after 5 years;
- option to defer dividend/coupon for up to 20 quarters without triggering a default;
- deferral option is subject to suspension of common dividend (if any);

3 By using a trust structure, issuers receive a tax deduction for interest payments made on the underlying subordinated loan. At the same time, the instrument appears on the balance sheet in the category between debt and equity, which gives the appearance of a more equity-like instrument. However, in its recent work on the Liabilities and Equity project, the Financial Accounting Standards Board (FASB) tentatively concluded that trust preferred securities should be classified as debt for accounting purposes.

- deferred amounts are cumulative and also accrue interest;
- all accrued amounts must be paid before resuming payment of the common dividend or at end of the limited deferral period.

No maturity – This instrument does not come significantly closer to replicating equity's 'no maturity' requirement than would an issue of traditional long-term debt. This would appear to hold for all issuers, regardless of industry and position on the credit spectrum.

In general, dated securities do not fully replicate the 'no maturity' characteristic embodied in common equity. The 40-year bullet payment in this example represents a cash outflow that is not scheduled to occur until far into the future, implying fairly nominal present value today. Nonetheless, it is still an obligation that the company must plan to repay from cash flow or refinance eventually. For a bank or other high-grade issuer, the security may not be much longer in duration than other long term obligations already extant.

As a debt claim, it is also an obligation that could become due immediately in the event of a default, cross default, bankruptcy filing or other form of reorganisation, which is particularly relevant for high-yield or lower investment grade issuers. The existence of the call option also raises the possibility that the instrument could be replaced in the future, with no guarantee that such an event will be neutral in its effect on other senior creditors.

No ongoing payments – The interest deferral option in trust preferred securities is a feature that has been borrowed from traditional preferred stock, and the degree of financial flexibility created is similar. For banks, financial institutions, and high-grade corporate issuers, the expectation at the time of issuance is that the feature is not likely to be used, because a failure to pay preferred dividends may sharply restrict the ability of these issuers to access the capital markets. Consequently, for such issuers, the security is considered a fixed-income obligation on the 'no ongoing payments' dimension of equity.

However, for lower investment-grade and high-yield issuers, the interest deferral feature is more likely to be used and therefore, better replicates equity on this dimension. The cumulative and accruing nature of the deferred payments is dissimilar to equity, and could result in a large cash payment in the future. However, the ability to defer payments for up to five years should be long enough to effectively bridge a potential extended period of financial stress and recovery.

Loss absorption – The underlying loan is legally subordinated in claim to all other debt of the parent, representing another feature that has been borrowed from traditional preferred stock. However, in terms of loss absorption, the subordinated debt claim is not identical to a true preferred claim. In a bankruptcy reorganisation, the subordinated creditor claim with its 'place at the negotiating table' could have a more senior claim than preferred stockholders have.

For these reasons, in terms of loss absorption, trust preferred securities do not replicate common equity, which has only a residual interest in bankruptcy and cannot trigger a default and put the company into bankruptcy. Clearly, loss absorption is less likely to be needed by high quality corporates and financial institutions, although the latter may derive some value from this feature in terms of complying with regulatory requirements. For lower quality issuers, however, there is greater potential that the subordination feature may serve as a practical protection for senior creditors.

Conclusion – As shown in the chart below, the features of trust preferred securities are not considered to replicate strongly the three principal characteristics of common equity, and the instrument is considered to be significantly more debt-like than equity-like for all issuers. However, the greater value of the interest deferral feature and the subordination of claim for high-yield issuers is recognised via the placement in Basket B rather than Basket A. (See Appendix 7.1 for position on the debt-equity continuum.)

Example – trust preferred securities

	Financial institutions	**High-grade corporates**	**Lower-rated corporates**
No maturity	None	None	None
No ongoing payments	None	None	Moderate
Loss absorption	None	None	Moderate
Continuum placement	**Basket A**	**Basket A**	**Basket B**

Hybrid securities issued by non-US companies that follow the basic trust preferred structure often have somewhat different characteristics than those issued by companies in the US. The instruments often have a perpetual maturity and the dividends may be tax-deductible, unlike in the US. In a liquidation, the holders may have a preferred stockholder's claim, rather than a debt holder's claim. For banks, the dividends and the liquidation preference may be subject to reduction if the bank's capital levels fall below certain regulatory ratios.

Mandatorily convertible preferred stock

From the issuer's perspective, mandatorily convertible preferred stock is a forward sale of common equity, with both cost and earnings dilution more or less fixed from the outset. Before conversion, which typically occurs in 3 to 5 years, the instrument provides financial flexibility similar to that of traditional preferred stock. The key features of these securities are as follows:

- preferred stock security, subordinated to all debt obligations and on parity with other directly issued preferreds;
- fixed coupon, which is not tax deductible;
- automatically converts to a fixed number of common shares after 3 to 5 years;
- receives similar treatment as common shares in merger or consolidation event;
- dividend may be deferred, subject to suspension of the common dividend (if any);
- deferred amounts typically are cumulative, and may or may not accrue interest;
- no requirement to pay deferred amounts prior to conversion, but must be paid before resuming common dividend;
- non-callable.

No maturity – Because this security automatically converts to common equity, at issuance it is considered to replicate closely common stock on the 'no maturity' dimension of equity. The instrument should never result in a repayment claim against the cash flow of the 'going concern' issuer.

No ongoing payments – Because the preferred dividends will be eliminated upon conversion, this type of security replicates common equity closely with regard to 'no ongoing payments'. More equity benefit is assigned to instruments that convert in three years, rather than five, because the ongoing payments are eliminated earlier. However, a mandatorily convertible preferred is not the same as common equity because any deferred dividends are typically cumulative and must be paid before the common dividend is resumed. In addition, the preferred dividend yield is usually substantially higher than the common dividend yield,[4] and in all but the most distressed circumstances, it is expected to be paid from the issuer's cash flow.

Loss absorption – Between the issuance date and the conversion date, the security represents a preferred claim, which is subordinated to all debt obligations and *pari passu* with other directly issued preferreds; after conversion, it is a common stock claim. In addition, under a merger or

4 The higher yield on mandatorily convertible preferred securities relative to the dividend on an issuer's common stock compensates the holder for receiving only part of the common stock price appreciation (beyond a certain threshold price, the holder receives a specified percentage of a share at conversion).

consolidation, which results in the distribution of cash or securities to the issuer's common stockholders, the mandatorily convertible preferred stock normally receives similar treatment.

The instrument provides a loss-absorbing cushion for senior creditors, and replicates common equity on this dimension. The loss absorption feature applies to all issuers, for different reasons. For high-grade issuers, it is highly probable that the security will be converted into common equity. For high-yield corporates, which have a higher probability of encountering financial distress before the conversion date, the preferred nature of the claim can provide more benefit in difficult situations.

Conclusion – As noted in the chart below, mandatorily convertible preferred securities receive high marks on all three dimensions of equity, and for all issuers, they are placed in basket E. Furthermore, as the conversion date approaches, the aggregate value of the remaining dividends declines and the likelihood that the new equity will remain a permanent part of the capital structure becomes more evident through our ongoing discussions with management.

Example – mandatorily convertible preferred stock

	Financial institutions	**High-grade corporates**	**Lower-rated corporates**
No maturity	Strong	Strong	Strong
No ongoing payments	Moderate	Moderate	Strong
Loss absorption	Strong	Strong	Strong
Continuum placement	**Basket E**	**Basket E**	**Basket E**

See Appendix 7.2 for position on debt-equity continuum.

Section 4: The impact of hybrid securities on an issuer's credit quality

The Tool Kit is the analytical framework that Moody's uses to place a hybrid security in a basket on the debt–equity continuum. This relative ranking of a hybrid security's debt and equity characteristics provides broad guidance as to the impact, if any, the instrument may have on an issuer's capital structure. However, capital structure is only one of the many factors that Moody's considers in its determination of ratings.

Depending on the overall strength of an issuer and the industry in which it operates, the level of capital – and more specifically, the component of common equity in the capital structure – may vary in its impact on an issuer's credit fundamentals. For example, one company may have high levels of common equity, but its profitability is steadily eroding. If the erosion is due to declining business trends, over time, the cushion available to support a changing business environment may diminish. Conversely, another company with average capital levels, but increasing earnings and a positive outlook for growth in its market share, may be a stronger credit than the 'well capitalised' one with diminishing returns.

Capital structures today tend to be less permanent than they were in the past for several reasons. Share repurchases have become a more regular occurrence and consequently, common stock may not have the permanence it once had. Hybrid securities seek to mimic the relative permanence of common stock, but they may have certain features that allow the instrument to be repaid with cash. Moreover, the substitution of one form of capital for another by an issuer can be a powerful signal of its view of the trade-off between shareholder and debt holder interests.

While capital substitution may have short-term equity benefits, it is really the evolution of the capital structure over time that is important. Moody's is most concerned with whether or not the capital structure provides adequate cushion to support the responses to a rapidly changing competitive environment that are necessary to preserve and/or enhance the issuer's cash generating capabilities.

Moody's also considers the hybrid security's role in the long-term financial strategy of the issuer and management's rationale for choosing the instrument over other alternatives. The company's anticipated use of the proceeds is also important and is analysed for consistency with stated business goals and for the creation of value. For example, does the company plan to use the hybrids to:

- Replace more expensive forms of capital, such as higher-coupon debt or non-tax deductible preferred stock?
- Replace shorter-term debt with longer-term securities?
- Invest in plant and equipment?
- Finance a major acquisition?
- Fund a stock buyback?

All these factors provide some insight into management's intent regarding the use of the instrument and composition of the capital structure in the future.

In addition to the capital structure, other factors considered in reaching a rating opinion are the issuer's competitive position, its franchise, and the industry dynamics, which provide insight into the future challenges that a company may face in its businesses. Asset quality and available sources of liquidity are also examined. **A company's ability to generate sustainable earnings, to increase its profitability, and to position its businesses for future growth – to ensure a steady source of earnings and cash flow to cover its financial obligations as they become due – play a key role in credit analysis.** Finally, the quality of management is an important factor in the determination of ratings.

Section 5: A case study

In order to illustrate how Moody's might factor a hybrid security into the rating opinion, a hypothetical example is provided.

Issuer A, which has a senior debt rating of A2, is a leading manufacturer of industrial equipment with strong market positions worldwide. Over the last few years, the company has improved the stability of its earnings and cash flows by diversifying geographically and by acquiring several businesses that respond to different phases of the economic cycles, thereby reducing the impact of a downturn in any one market.

The issuer's management team has a strong track record for identifying and successfully integrating acquisitions, some of which have been large. Although the issuer may increase its debt levels to fund an acquisition, it has consistently used excess cash flow and proceeds from asset sales to repay debt according to projections, restoring its financial measurements in a timely manner to a level that is consistent with the rating category.

To diversify further its business mix, Issuer A decides to make a significant acquisition, its largest to date. The acquisition target is a market leader in a business that is only somewhat related to the businesses of Issuer A (there is similarity in terms of suppliers, manufacturing process, technology, and distribution). The target has historically good cash flow generation through the cycles, and the earnings prospects are generally favourable for the next several years, despite the company's exposure to Asian markets.

The acquisition is financed by a combination of traditional debt (requiring ongoing interest payments and the payment of principal in full at maturity) and a hybrid security. The hybrid security, which accounts for approximately 20% of the financing package, is a 5-year trust preferred combined with a 3-year forward purchase contract resulting in the issuance of equity. After applying Moody's Tool Kit to the instrument, it is placed in basket D.

While recognising the financial flexibility that the hybrid security creates, the credit analysis focuses on the size of the acquisition and the 80% of the purchase price financed with straight debt, which significantly weakens the issuer's financial and debt-protection measurements. The discussion centres on Issuer A's ability to reduce its significant debt load over the next few years. What is different with this acquisition is that Issuer A is relying solely on its operating cash flow to repay debt – no asset sales are contemplated. The concern is that the issuer's other businesses may weaken with an anticipated downturn in its markets before any meaningful debt reduction can be accomplished. Moreover, the rating committee considers the likelihood that the hybrid security, which will eventually result in the issuance of equity, will remain a permanent part of the capital structure.

The rating committee decides to lower the senior debt rating one notch to A3 despite high debt levels and initially weakened cash flow and debt-protection measurements that suggest a lower rating. Management's track record for successfully integrating acquisitions and reducing acquisition-related debt in a timely manner is a significant factor in the rating decision. It is also anticipated that management will limit any future acquisition activity until its balance sheet strengthens. Finally, it is noted that the company has not made any significant share repurchases over the last several years.

Section 6: Conclusion

This Rating Methodology provides the analytical framework used by Moody's to place a particular hybrid security on the debt–equity continuum. To accomplish this task, the instrument is first broken down into its basic features including maturity, call option, conversion features, deferral features, and its priority of claim in bankruptcy. These features are then compared to the characteristics of pure equity – no maturity, no promised ongoing payments that could trigger a default if unpaid, cushion in bankruptcy for all creditors – to see how closely the features replicate equity.

Moody's determines the relative weight of the instrument's characteristics and then places the instrument in one of five baskets ranging from A to E on the debt–equity continuum. By stripping out all issuer-specific considerations, the continuum provides a generic ranking for hybrid securities on a relative basis and a determination of their potential impact on the capital structure at the issuance date.

Still, the relative ranking of hybrid securities provided by their placement on the debt–equity continuum is only a starting point in the determination of the ratings impact, if any, for a particular issuer. Once the characteristics of the hybrid security are assessed, the instrument is viewed within the context of each issuer's overall credit fundamentals. In many instances, the instruments in and of themselves do not make a difference in the rating outcome.

Moody's always considers a company's capital structure in assessing its credit fundamentals, but capital is by no means the sole consideration and, in fact, it is probably not the most important factor. How a company positions itself to generate earnings and cash flow – the steps that it takes to secure its future, including business investments, capital spending, and acquisitions, and how these investments are financed – form the primary basis for a rating opinion. Consequently, Moody's focuses on the effect that a hybrid security will have on a company's cash flow, when it evaluates the potential benefits that the company may obtain from using the hybrid.

Appendix 7.1

Hybrid security

Trust preferred security

Position on debt–equity continuum

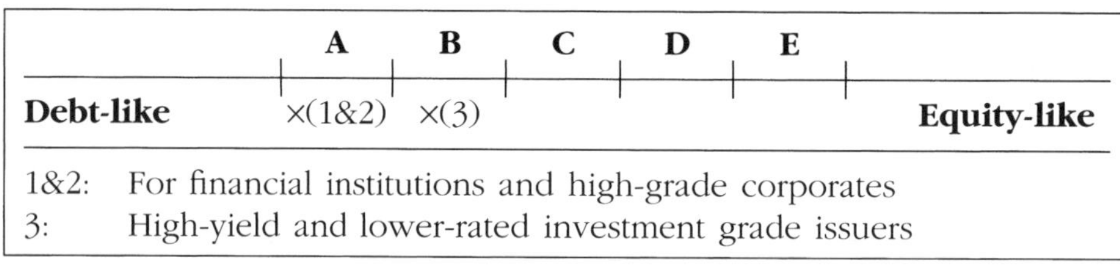

Description/main features

Under a trust preferred structure, preferred securities are issued by a trust, which lends proceeds to the parent company through a subordinated loan that is junior to all other debt of the parent. The terms of the preferred securities match the terms of the underlying subordinated loan. The parent makes tax-deductible interest payments sufficient to cover dividend payments, and also guarantees, on a subordinated basis, the payment of principal and dividends to the extent that there are funds in the trust. The other key features are:

- Long maturity (for example, a 40-year bullet).
- Callable after 5 years.
- Option to defer dividend payments for up to 5 years without triggering a default.

- Deferral option is subject to a suspension of the common dividend.
- Deferred amounts are cumulative and accrue interest.
- All accrued amounts must be paid before resuming payment of the common dividend or at the end of the limited deferral period.

Analysis of features

No maturity – In general, dated securities do not fully replicate the 'no maturity' characteristic of common equity. Despite the fairly nominal present value of a 40-year obligation today, it is an obligation that the company must plan to pay from cash flow or refinance eventually. As a debt claim, it is also an obligation that could become due immediately in the event of a default, cross default, or bankruptcy filing, which has more relevance for high-yield issuers. The existence of the call option also raises the possibility that the instrument could be replaced in the future with no guarantee that such event will be neutral in its effect on other senior creditors.

No ongoing payments – For banks, financial institutions, and high-grade corporate issuers, the expectation at the time of issuance is that the interest deferral feature is not likely to be used because a failure to pay preferred dividends may sharply restrict the ability of these issuers to access the capital markets. For such issuers, the security is considered a fixed income obligation. However, for lower investment-grade and high-yield issuers, the interest deferral feature is more likely to be used and creates additional flexibility at a time of financial distress.

Loss absorption – While the underlying subordinated loan between the trust and the parent company is junior to all other debt of the parent company, the subordinated creditor claim with its 'place at the negotiating table' could have a more senior claim than preferred stockholders. As a result, the instrument has less ability to absorb losses than does common equity.

Equity replication summary (at issuance)

(Strong, Moderate, Weak, or None relative to debt)

	Financial institutions	**High-grade corporates**	**Lower-rated corporates**
No maturity	None	None	None
No ongoing payments	None	None	Moderate
Loss absorption	None	None	Moderate
Basket	**A**	**A**	**B**

Appendix 7.2

Hybrid security

Mandatorily convertible preferred stock

Position on debt–equity continuum

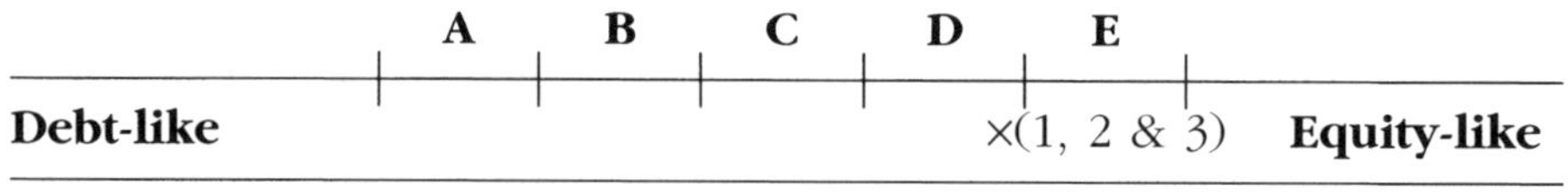

1&2: For financial institutions and high-grade corporates
3: High-yield and lower-rated investment grade issuers

Description/main features

From the issuer's perspective, mandatorily convertible preferred stock is a forward sale of common equity with both cost and earnings dilution fixed from the outset. The key features of the security are:

- Preferred stock, which is subordinated to all debt obligations and on parity with other directly issued preferred securities.
- Fixed coupon, which is not tax deductible.
- Automatically converts to a fixed number of shares after 3 years.
- Receives similar treatment as common shares in a merger or consolidation event.
- Dividends may be deferred, subject to suspension of the common dividend.
- Deferred amounts are cumulative and may or may not accrue interest.
- There is no requirement to pay the deferred amounts prior to conversion, but the amounts must be paid before resuming the common dividend.
- Non-callable.

Analysis of features

No maturity – Because the security automatically converts to common equity, it is considered to replicate closely the 'no maturity' dimension of equity. The instrument will not result in a repayment claim against the cash flow of the 'going concern' issuer.

No ongoing payments – Because the preferred dividends may be deferred for its effective life, this type of security also replicates the 'no ongoing payments' dimension of equity closely. However, it is not the same as common equity because the deferred amounts are typically cumulative and must be repaid before the common dividend is resumed. In addition, the preferred dividend yield is usually substantially higher than the common dividend yield, and in all but the most distressed circumstances, it is expected to be paid from the issuer's cash flow.

Loss absorption – Between the issuance date and the conversion date, the security represents a preferred claim, which is subordinated to all debt obligations and is *pari passu* with other directly issued preferred securities; after conversion, it is a common stock claim. The instrument provides a loss-absorbing cushion for the senior creditors of all issuers, but is most relevant for high-yield issuers.

Equity replication summary (at issuance)

(Strong, Moderate, Weak, or None relative to debt)

	Financial institutions	**High-grade corporates**	**Lower-rated corporates**
No maturity	Strong	Strong	Strong
No ongoing payments	Moderate	Moderate	Strong
Loss absorption	Strong	Strong	Strong
Basket	**E**	**E**	**E**

Appendix 7.3

Hybrid security

Five-year trust preferred security combined with three-year equity forward purchase contract

Position on debt–equity continuum

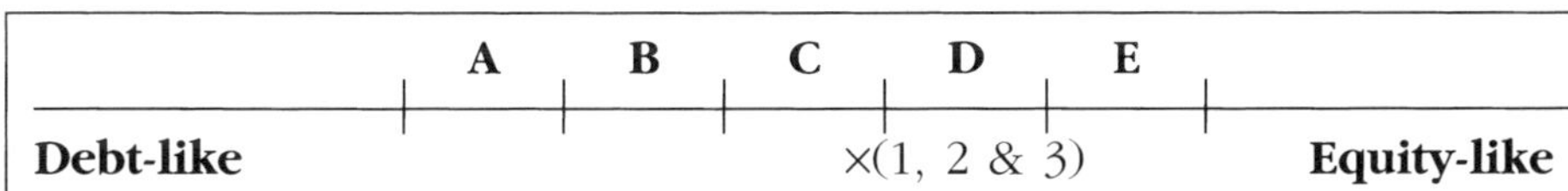

1&2: For financial institutions and high-grade corporates
3: High-yield and lower-rated investment grade issuers

Description/main features

In this combination of instruments, a 5-year trust preferred security is combined with a 3-year equity forward purchase contract. The investor holds a trust preferred security and a piece of the forward purchase contract. In year 3, the investor has two options. Either the investor exchanges the trust preferred security for the company's common stock and the company remarkets the trust preferred security for the remaining 2 years, or the investor pays cash for the common stock and holds onto the trust preferred security for its remaining life. In either case, the company receives new equity and additional cash in year 3.

The purchase contract is for a fixed number of shares, resulting in the transfer of stock price downside risk to the investor and known EPS dilution for the issuer. In addition, the purchase contract is binding, notwithstanding interim debt default or a bankruptcy filing by the issuer. The analysis assumes that the cash received in year 3 is used for debt reduction so that the trust preferred, which remains outstanding for 2 additional years, does not represent incremental debt. Moreover, if the equity remains a permanent part of the capital structure, this combination of instruments replicates the equity benefit of mandatorily convertible preferred stock.

Analysis of features

No maturity – Although the trust preferred security represents a debt-like instrument with a 5-year maturity, the equity forward purchase contract is intended to ensure a repayment source other than the company's cash flow. However, this assumes that the company uses the cash received in year 3 to repay outstanding debt such that the trust preferred, which remains outstanding for another 2 years, does not represent incremental debt.

No ongoing payments – A fixed dividend is payable on the trust preferred, but is deferrable for the life of the instrument at management's option, subject to the simultaneous suspension of common dividends. Passed dividends are cumulative, accrue interest, and are not covered by the exercise of the equity forward purchase contract. This option is not likely to be used by financial institutions and high-grade corporates due to reputation and confidence sensitivity concerns, but may provide flexibility for high-yield issuers. There is a also a small fixed contract fee payable by the issuer on the forward purchase contract.

Loss absorption – Trust preferred securities have a subordinated debt claim, which could impact senior debt recovery in the event of a bankruptcy filing. However, given the short term until equity proceeds are received, this is not a concern for high-grade issuers although it could be a concern for high-yield issuers.

Equity replication summary (at issuance)

(Strong, Moderate, Weak, or None relative to debt)	**Financial institutions**	**High-grade corporates**	**Lower-rated corporates**
No maturity	Strong	Strong	Moderate
No ongoing payments	Weak	Weak	Moderate
Loss absorption	Weak	Weak	Moderate
Basket	**D**	**D**	**D**

Index